How to Ditch the Bitch

Winning the Inner Game of Transformation

Leanne Ellington

Dedicated

to all the women that have *Bitches* in their lives.

Before You Begin:

PART 1: The Bitch Life

Part 2: How to Speak Fluent Bitch

Forward

It's not every day that you come across an idea so obvious, so simple and yet so powerfully impactful as those presented within the pages of this short book.

What you now hold in your hands is a truly powerful antidote to all of the naysaying, negative, and downright nasty things that you've most likely been saying TO yourself ABOUT yourself for as long as you can remember. Things related to how you look (or don't look), how smart (or dumb) you are, how gifted (or untalented) you feel, how valued (or worthless) you rate yourself to be and, in fact, every single horrible, nasty or downright bitchy judgment or comment you've ever thought or said about yourself.

Much more than a simple 'be kind to yourself' or 'believe you're worth it' platitude offered by so many others working within the women's self-help genre, this little gem goes deeper by drawing on the latest findings in neuroscience as it relates to self-confidence, self-perception and self-esteem and helps women who are struggling to create change to finally rid themselves of the guilt, shame, and failure labels that are keeping them stuck where they are and living lives they don't love.

Written in a clean, clear and highly consumable format, the book speaks to women in language they will understand and simply 'get' right from the start. By transforming negative thoughts, words and actions from a 'mindset thing' thing to the personalization of their qualities through 'The Bitches', women will finally come to understand why they feel the way they do, where those feelings come from and, perhaps most importantly, what to do about them in order to create rapid yet long-lasting change.

In creating *How To Ditch The Bitch*, coach Leanne Ellington has undoubtedly created a giant leap for womankind that will certainly be marked as a turning point in moving women from living lives that they loathe to experiencing lives that they love.

As a coach myself and educator to coaches worldwide I can offer no greater testament to Leanne's *How To Ditch The Bitch* philosophies than to say that if you read the book cover to cover, do the exercises as laid out by Leanne and take the subsequent actions based upon what you find, a better life is not just possible or even probable. It's guaranteed!

Now... go ditch those bitches!

Dax Moy
Author of The Magic 100

Meet the Bitches

I've yet to come across a single woman that didn't have them.

The negative self-talk, the limiting beliefs in your head, the perfectionists in your mind that will never feel like you are 'enough'.

They are the Bitches. At least that's what I call them.

If you've ever had a voice in your head at some point or another saying you're too this or not enough that.

That's a Bitch.

If you've ever made one of those snide, judgmental, perfectionist remarks that we make to ourselves when we have the *shoulda's*, the *woulda's*, or the *coulda's*.

That's a Bitch.

And I believe we all have them.

Some have more than others, and some have them show up more frequently than others, but I believe we all do indeed have them.

And it's my mission to at least tell as many women as I can that they exist.

Simply knowing about 'The Bitches' will change the way you think about almost every area of your life and help you identify the road blocks that are currently (for whatever reason) keeping you feeling stuck or simply making you feel less than you want to feel.

MY Bitches:

My Bitches almost kept me from ever releasing the words on this page.

They told me:

> "It's not ready yet."

> "There's too many typos."

> "They won't like it."

> "Do they really give a sh*t what YOU think?"

> "Who are you to be an author?"

> "What gives you the right to tell women how to change their lives?"

There were so many things that my Bitches have said to me over the years. They really did a number on me.

So warts, typos, and all, here I am, and here is *How to Ditch the Bitch.*

I'm not pretending it's perfect. Heck I can't even claim that it's complete. There is so much I could share with you about the Bitches, and so many personal anecdotes I could reflect on.

But for purposes of this book, I've told my *Perfectionist Bitch* and my *Typo Bitch* to take a hike and let me do my thing.

Consider this book a medley of *Bitchery*: personal anecdotes, random rambles, analogies (some better than others), and of course a system -- YOUR system for *Bitch-Ditchery*.

YOUR Bitches:

Okay so if you are anything like me, you've probably been around the self-improvement and transformation "block" a time or two. This isn't your first book or your first rodeo.

So allow me to address any of YOUR Bitches that may appear along the way.

> *"Really? you think some book is gonna change anything?"*

> *"You've tried 1000 things. How is this any different?"*

> *"Okay, this is just going to be one more book you read half-way through and then forget about. "*

> *"Great! Yup! I've got Bitches alright. But they've been around my whole life, so what's the point? "*

Truth is: Typically you would be right...about all of it.

But I assure you that you have never seen yourself or your struggles in this light before.

Once you understand that you aren't "weak-willed", you don't lack motivation or willpower, and that it's not a matter of "this is just the way I am", you won't be singing the same tune.

So get cozy and get ready. It's time for YOU to tell your own Bitches to take a hike.

This Book

This book is a product of the last 20 years of my life. Would things have been a lot smoother and easier if I had the future version of myself walking around with my present self every day? Of course it would have. But it wouldn't have enabled me to write the words on this page.

Imagine if you could clone yourself and send yourself back in time to give advice to your younger self. Keep that thought in mind as you go through this tale, because I truly believe that in a way you can.

Even the parts of you that have been around for as long as you can remember.

Even the parts of you that you summed up as "that's just how I am".

Even the things that have given you the most trouble over the years.

I believe that you can very quickly and easily let go of those stories you have about yourself that are holding you back—the same ones that are keeping you STUCK – and *Ditch* them.

You'll hear me referring to my younger self throughout this book, but it's my invitation for you to see where some of the things I share may be showing up in YOUR life.

I've worked with, mentored, and encountered 1000's of women over the years, and I wanted to make sure that I addressed the most important questions I have been asked about the principles I plan to share with you here.

In doing so, you'll also hear me describe two different variations of the same situation—one where *Bitchery* takes over, and one where *Ditchery* is in the mix.

- ★ **The *Bitchery* Version**: How things went down in my life
- ★ **The *Ditchery* Version**: The way things could have gone down if I had sent my *Bitch-Detecting* self back in time to help my younger self see what she didn't see.

It's my hope to save you the time, frustration, and resistance that I went through before I became increasingly aware of the *Bitches* that were showing up in my life.

I've found that a lot of times when women aren't happy in one area of their life, it becomes this trickling cascade of doubt in other areas of their life as well.

Often it means that self-confidence and self-esteem go right out the window.

So what do confident women with high self-esteem know that the rest don't know?

Contrary to popular belief my experience has shown me that it actually has little to do with what you're doing (or not doing).

What makes a difference is HOW you do what you do – who you are **be**ing as you go about the 'business' of your life.

Focusing on who you are **be**ing instead of what you are **do**ing is the way to love who you are being AND what you are doing.

- ★ It's the difference between knowing what to do and getting yourself to do it.

- ★ It's the difference between doing something because you think you "should" and doing something because it lights you up and pumps you up.
- ★ It's the difference between going in whatever direction life's momentum seems to be carrying you and going in whatever direction you really WANT to go.
- ★ It's the difference between having the relationships you **have** and having the relationships you **want**.

The problem is that most women spend their time focusing on what they need to **do** instead of spending it working on becoming the kind of woman that would have THAT life.

The kind of woman that would walk as confidently and gracefully as you would like to walk. How would she talk to herself? How would she feel about herself?

The kind of woman that would speak up whenever she had something to say or contribute, and would make it a point to say what she means and mean what she says. How would she talk to herself? How would she feel about herself?

The kind of woman that would have a nicely-kept and well-organized home, or the best relationships she could possibly want for herself, or the work life that keeps her inspired and makes her proud. How would she live her life?

How would she be spending her time?

How would she NOT be spending her time?

I have discovered that the women that feel confident and powerful within themselves have a few things in common:

- ★ They talk to themselves a certain way.
- ★ They DON'T talk to themselves a certain way.
- ★ The do very specific things in their everyday life.
- ★ They DON'T do very specific things in their everyday life.

And that is the main purpose of this book. I want to help you find THAT. I want to help you identify that way of living as it pertains to your life.

Then no matter what you are seeking—anything from weight loss to jumping ahead in your career to having loving and happy relationships—you would have the beliefs and habits and confidence of the person that would go make THAT happen.

Then on top of that, I want to help you learn how to make sure that every plan-of-attack you commit to is designed (from the very beginning) to be a "Winning Game". You'll learn why setting yourself up for a "Losing Game" is a surefire way to make sure that YOUR Bitches are always right alongside you.

But before we go any further, allow me to tell you exactly what I mean when I use the word *Bitch*.

BITCH – The nagging voice in your head that you're not *enough*.
DITCH – Not allowing her to run your life for one more minute.

At its simplest, *Bitchery* is the negative self-talk and unfair self-judgment that we may have acquired over the years—the same ones that keep us feeling down on ourselves, disappointed, or disempowered. And that is what is this book was designed to help you eliminate.

The act of *Ditching* simply means choosing not to be impacted by these *stories of self* any longer and making sure that YOU are the one holding the steering wheel of your life. Even if your inner-*Bitches* are around, they don't have to run your life.

The mission of *Ditch the Bitch* is to provide a framework of language you can pull from in order to (a) feel *in control* of your life and (b) talk to yourself like you would talk to someone you LOVE (or at least are learning to love).

And it is my personal mission to help you sift through and figure out all the beliefs and habits that you don't want anymore, that aren't serving your life—and then Ditch them.

Then with a clean, relaxed mind, I want to help you figure out some new stories and definitions that WOULD serve your best life.

I plan to give you a new framework and pair of goggles with which to see your life and to live by. The language I have to teach, if you use it, can get you anything you want.

On the next page is a closer look at how the word *Bitch* could show up in your everyday world.

Bitch: (n),(v)

1. The naysayer or "dealmaker" that takes you off-road whenever you set out to do or accomplish something; The saboteur that reinforces your bad habits, making it easy to make excuses.

Example: You don't feel like exercising today. Just stay home. One day off won't make a difference. Keep your butt on the couch, you can clean tomorrow.

2. Inner-critic that makes you question yourself, your abilities, or your judgment, or tells you that you're not ___enough.

Example: You aren't smart enough for that job, don't bother applying. You're not pretty enough for that guy, he wouldn't give you the time of day.

3. The voice inside that tells you to quit or makes it okay NOT to finish what you start.

Example: You promised yourself you would practice guitar every day this month and you've already missed two days. You weren't really making any progress anyway. Time to throw in the towel.

4. The unfair judgmental voices that label who you are based on what you do.

Example:
You ate more cheesecake than you should have, you're a fat ass.
You goofed on a project at work. You're an idiot.
You didn't leave a sweet note in your kid's lunchbox today. You're a bad mom.

5. Complaining about the things you have the power to change; not accept ownership of your own life and circumstances.

Example:
You know you aren't doing your best, but you still choose to complain about it. It's everyone else's fault that you aren't happy.

Synonyms: Meanie, hater, naysayer, second-guesser, judge, critic, frenemy, abuser, tormentor, bully, shamer, blamer, regretter, deal-maker, adversary, rival, negative influence, instigator, troublemaker, competitor, broken record, know-it-all, energy vampire, pessimist, threat, voice of your insecurities, the voice of your fears.

Why Most Self-Help Doesn't Work

No doubt you heard the following statement (in song-like fashion) growing up:

"First comes love. Then comes marriage. Then comes the baby in the baby carriage."

Remember that one?

It's cute. It's memorable. But it's not REALLY how life works.

There's this whole 'courting' process that goes on before anyone even thinks about throwing out the L-word.

It should really go:

First comes LIKE, then comes LOVE (and then you can have your happily ever after).

And this doesn't just go for finding a partner or the love of your life. It starts right back at the very beginning....with YOU.

Let's look at this from the *Ditch the Bitch* perspective for just a moment:

If there's something in your life that you don't love-- anything you don't love about yourself, your body, your lifestyle-- there's most likely the voice of one of YOUR *Bitches* whispering in your ear and reminding you of this fact.

You don't just (POOF!) magically start loving your body or yourself because you sat down and read a book about self-love or watched a Tony Robbins documentary.

Just like they say in business, you first need to KNOW, LIKE, & TRUST someone before you do business with them. It's not different when it comes to 'doing business' with yourself.

And this is where I believe self-help and personal development drop the ball.

You can find a million books or programs that talk about learning to truly love yourself (trust me, I own a lot of them). But I've yet to come across one that mentions this one important factor when it comes to self-love:

The Know, Like, Trust Factor.

Learning to 'love yourself' is fine and dandy if that's the natural next progression, but for a lot of women 'looking for love', it's not.

I set out on my own *Ditch the Bitch* journey after I realized how downright Bitchy I was being to myself-- when I realized that my Bitches were not saying the niiiicest things to me. (Insert: understatement of the century)

And looking back, it was specifically when it came to those areas that I didn't KNOW, LIKE, or TRUST my body, myself, or my lifestyle (habits, routines, etc.).

It's no wonder my road to self-love was so curvy and bumpy. I skipped the first steps!

Let's look at your Bitchery through another lens for just a moment.

★ The language of the Bitch is FEAR
★ The opposite of FEAR is LOVE
★ LOVE is comprised of KNOW LIKE TRUST

It's a bit of a different kind of 'math', isn't it? But it's one that I believe will change your life if you step into it.

And don't worry if you're thinking to yourself: *"Oh great! I don't know myself, like myself, OR trust myself! I'm screwed!"*
Don't worry my friend. I used to think the same thing about myself and my own struggles.

But nothing could be further from the truth.

I say this now, and I believe it with my whole heart:

It's never too late to go become someone else.

It's never too late to go become the version of yourself you always wanted to become, but never knew was possible.

It's never too late to realize that you already ARE her, even if you haven't seen her in a very long time. She lives within you already.

But it doesn't mean completely abandoning everything you've become since the day you were born either.

Don't throw away the baby with the bathwater.

Keep the amazing parts – – the parts you are proud of and the parts that make you more YOU -- that make you beautiful.

If you don't know what those are, find them. Keep them. And keep reminding yourself of them every single day...

And then ditch the rest. Ditch the parts that aren't serving you. Ditch the parts that aren't making you happy.

Chisel away the parts of you that you never created, and don't want to spend your whole life carrying around.

It's NEVER too late to become you really are.

"I saw an angel in the block of marble and I just chiseled 'til I set him free." **-- Michelangelo**

But the story you tell yourself will only change when you decide that it MUST.

The story will only change as you begin to KNOW yourself truthfully 'naked'.

As you come to know your 'warts and all' self, you will start to LIKE yourself.

As you engage in activities that support your growing like, you will have the opportunity to see, make, and keep promises.

This will create TRUST.

As the trust 'bank account' builds up, you will grow to love yourself as honest, trustworthy, kind, likeable...and this will develop into LOVE.

There can be no other path to love.

It's a road of acceptance, connection, and care.

It's a journey through know, like, and trust.

And I want every woman to know what life is like down this road.

Remember:
★ The language of the Bitch is FEAR
★ The opposite of FEAR is LOVE
★ LOVE is comprised of KNOW LIKE TRUST

No matter what you currently believe, for every woman who is a slave to her thoughts, feelings, and actions, the reality is that your 'enemy' is within.

But your enemy isn't REALLY your enemy, she's a scared little girl...or the parts of you that never grew up... or the voice inside of you screaming at you to find a better way.

Those voices are what are keeping you feeling stuck and scared. And the voices will make sense when you learn to speak their language.

The things you want are MUCH closer that you think, but you won't get any closer if you don't change WHAT you think.

And the story you tell yourself will only change when you decide that it MUST.

Another Self Help Book?

Does the world need another how-to or self-help book? I'm going to venture to say no. But in the world of how-to's, I believe there is a fatal flaw to every single one of them:

All of them are great in theory. In fact they might be OVERFLOWING with the best of the best in knowledge, research, and on-the-ground tactical blueprints or action plans.

It may have been one you found for free on Pinterest, or it could be the most expensive how-to you've ever paid to get access to.

But none of that makes a difference. I mean what good is the best-of-the-best or the cream-of-the-crop if you can't get yourself to actually **do** it? What good would it do you if you can't get yourself to **live** by it?

I started my career in the health and fitness 'world'. And honestly even before a client of mine lost (or didn't lose) a single pound or inch, and without taking a look at what they were (or weren't) eating, I could tell pretty quickly whether or not that client was going to get long-term results with my programs.

All I had to do was watch their patterns and take note of the way they talked **to** themselves and **about** themselves.

- ★ Did they talk like they actually believed in themselves and thought they could see it through to the end?
- ★ Did they have excuses for EVERYTHING?
- ★ Did they put themselves down or speak of themselves unkindly?
- ★ Did they make it a point to follow through on the promises they made to themselves?

There's no shortage of how-to-do-this or how-to-do-that books or articles. Between "University of Google" and Dr. Facebook, you can essentially get your hands on all the information you could ever need about the "what to do" part of anything. Knowledge is not the problem here.

Getting yourself to actually **do it** is the big struggle that we all face. Getting ourselves to take the necessary actions to get the job done is where most people fall short.

And don't get me wrong, pushing yourself past your own limits and doing the "work" is not easy. In fact it might feel like the hardest thing you'd ever done in your life. And it will test you, make you want to quit, and push you into the face of resistance.

But it's what you say **to** yourself and **about** yourself when you start to struggle, when you get off course, or when you feel like giving up that make the difference in it all.

That is where that confident and self-assured woman I referred to earlier sees the world differently. But I guarantee you she didn't become this way by accident.

Eliminating that inner-critic or naysaying voice in your head that is convincing you to do or not do the things you want to do is tough.

Those voices in your head that are keeping you stuck—the ones that are sabotaging your motivation, your willpower, or stealing your smiles — those are *the Bitches* that I'm referring to.

If you want to create change — and I mean long-lasting transformational change -- it comes down to eliminating the wrath of *the Bitches* in your life and making sure that they don't hold the power any longer.

PART 1:
THE BITCH LIFE

If you recorded your inner most thoughts throughout the day, and you had to categorize your inner self-talk into three categories, it might look like this:

1. Words that sound like they are coming from your biggest critic, the mean girl, the bully, or your worst enemy

2. Words your best friend, your biggest fan, and your biggest cheerleader would say to you

3. Words of your Frenemy. Not your enemy, but certainly not your friend. She's indifferent. She's a bystander (which can sometimes be even more harmful).

Which category do you think would have the most tick boxes?

Where do YOU have bitches showing up in your life?

Telling you how you should feel about your body...
Telling you how you should feel about your relationships...
Guiding your internal thoughts—telling you whether or not to go after what you truly want.

Can you imagine what your life would be like if you simply cut out all the *Bitches* in your life and just decided you weren't going to listen to them any longer?

What would happen if you no longer let those voices boss you around, beat you down, or make you feel like you don't deserve any more out of your life than you're already living?

What would happen if you simply decided to *Ditch the Bitch*?

Think about the next time you set out to lose a few pounds, go after that job that you *really* want, or to simply 'upgrade' your life in any of the ways you want to.

Just imagine what your life would be like if YOUR *Bitches* weren't around to tell you:

> *"You might as well just give up now; you don't have a shot at succeeding."*
> *"That job is going to go to that prettier, skinnier, gal—you should just back out now."*
> *"He'll never love you with THOSE thighs, THAT hair, or THAT squeaky-sounding voice of yours."*
> *"What's WRONG with you??"*

Imagine if you woke up one day and suddenly all the *Bitches* in your life were gone (or no longer impacted you the same way).

★ No more *"I should have done this"* or *"I could have done that"*
★ No more, *"You're not (X) enough."*
★ No more name-calling and doubt-filled remarks

I know for me personally; it all came down to an awareness that all the Bitches in my life were showing up *everywhere*.

I used to look in the mirror and one of my inner-bitches would scour my reflection for anything and everything she could get her hands on to pick apart or look at with dismay.

I used to walk into a room and that inner-bitch of mine would tell me that it was going to be a mess—a complete disaster. That I was going to appear awkward or not fit in.

I used to think about my dreams and what I really want for my life, and of course, without a moment's delay, my inner-bitch would tell me it would *never happen*. That I should just *give up now* and *save myself the trouble or embarrassment.*

But the day I realized that these voices were around, and that they went EVERYWHERE that I went, my life changed.

You see, I pride myself in the fact that I don't hang around people that treat me like dirt, and I never have. As far back as 3rd grade, when a girl made fun of me because my shirt was from Ross Dress for Less instead of The Limited Too (yes, I remember this like it was yesterday), I remember giving her the ol' "screw you!" in my mind, and never looking back.

If I had a friend, love interest, co-worker, or any acquaintance who didn't treat me with love and kindness—the same love and kindness I show my friends and loved ones—it was easy for me to untangle myself from their hurtful webs.

So why did I continue to let the Bitches in my head continue to tear me down, abuse me, and continually let me feel like I was *less than*? That, my friend, is another story all on its own—one that I'll be sharing with you throughout this book.

But before I continue on, I want to nudge you to ask yourself throughout your reading:

Where do YOU have Bitches showing up in your life?

And what would your life look like if you simply decided to *Ditch the Bitch*?

The Prequel

You know how they came out with the first Star Wars movie, and then a few years later they came out with the Prequel to the first movie? Well I'm not 100% sure if Stephen Spielberg did that on purpose, but the same kind of thing happened to me.

Like I said earlier, I started out in the health and fitness industry quite a few years back after making over my own body. But if I knew then what I know now, my entire journey could have been a lot easier, and I could have enjoyed it a lot more.

You see, my mind (and my life really) were being run by my own personal Bitches.

So it's no surprise that having very little confidence in myself and being really overweight from a young age attracted my own unique set of *Mean Girls* running the show. My Bitches were constantly telling me I was fat, unattractive, or that I wasn't enough-- period.

Smart enough. Successful enough. You get the picture.

These Bitches stole my smiles, killed my confidence, and talked me out of going after what I really wanted.

Sometimes I think about what it would be like if I could zap my current self back in time ten years ago.

I would have pressed the pause button as soon as I got there though (in order to slow down for a moment) and teach my younger self a few important skills. I would have also immediately started teaching her the Language of the Bitches and what it all actually meant.

That way she would be equipped with as much Bitch-Detecting and Bitch-Ditching power as possible.

What they look like, where they show up, and what they could say at any moment that would put a damper on anything and everything.

- ★ Weight loss
- ★ Loving what you do everyday
- ★ Self-Esteem and Confidence
- ★ Relationships

Seriously, everything!

And I would be sure to let her know that having the Bitches running the show was NOT mandatory.

Ditch the Bitch is like the reality check that I wish someone would have given me years ago, or that I could go back and tell my younger self.

If I were writing the movie-version story of my life, I would definitely start with my own Prequel. It would go something like this:

(Insert James Earl Jones' voice reading it of course)

In a world where women struggle to feel confident, beautiful, powerful, and in control of their lives, a clique of women have come into the lives of ladies all over the world with one thing in mind:

Destroy every shred of self-belief, self-love, and self-confidence… and take control of their beliefs, habits, bodies, hopes, dreams, and happiness… one woman at a time.

These are The Bitches, and they will stop at nothing to steal your smiles, poke holes in your confidence, and keep you stuck for as long as they can.

Living the Bitch Life

When I was 7, my dad took me to Weight Watchers. He never told me I was fat. He never told me I was ugly or that I wasn't "enough". He simply took me to Weight Watchers.

I was the one who said I was fat.

I was the one who thought I was an embarrassment or something to be ashamed of.

I was the one who called myself a whole lot of names from a young age.

That's when it all started for me. From there on out I had Bitches running my self-talk, telling me who I was and who I wasn't, telling me what I was or wasn't capable of doing, and telling me that I wasn't good enough.

I grew up quite literally a *fat girl*— and I'm not even referring to topping the scales at nearly 250 pounds. That's not what I mean by *fat*. Everything else about me—inside and out-- was *fat* too.

My mindset was fat. My self-esteem was fat. My confidence was fat. My outlook on life was fat. And I don't mean that in a good way-- quite far from it actually. (See instead definition: *phat*)

What I'm saying is that every thought that entered my mind— every encounter I had with another human being, every endeavor in my life-- I viewed it all with blinders on. I viewed it with my *fat* head.

Trust me; this was no way to live.

Fast forward to today's world, I don't live like this anymore.

My personal Bitches did originally stem from my own "daddy issues", the "tough love" of my three older brothers, my desires to be perfect, my desires to fit in, and a whole slew of things that I'll share with you throughout these chronicles.

Those were the origins of course, but today my dad is one of my biggest fans, my biggest cheerleaders, and always telling me how beautiful I am and how proud he is of me.

The "tough love" from my brothers is now just love. We would all "take a bullet" for each other.
Perfectionism is no longer something I strive towards—or even think is a positive thing anymore.

And no longer will you catch me trying to blend in with the rest of the world or trying to 'be like' someone that I admire.

I just want to be me. My unshakeable self. Self-defined. Self-aware. Self-*loved*.

I went through my fair share of adversity over the years. Looking back I see that I was living inside of walls that I created and a prison of my own making, but I still went through major adversity.

But it wouldn't have mattered if I had a "perfect" upbringing or whether I was raised on the streets in a world of poverty. Bitches aren't circumstance-based beings. They are perception-based beings. Bitches come and go based on YOUR perception of the world, your life, and yourself.

The great news is that you can alter your perception and the way you see the world around you. The tricky part is that if you aren't careful, after a while, the Bitches can *become* your perception.

And that's why I believe it's your duty to get to know the Bitches. See how they live. See how they talk. Know where they show up. Know when they might be expected to arrive. And most importantly, know how to put the leash on them and take back ownership of your own life.

You see, I used to blame every**one** and every**thing** else for the fact that I didn't love myself and didn't love my life. Even decades later I realized I was **still** blaming my dad for something he did one time when I was 7 years old (taking me to Weight Watchers), and I could continue blaming him to this very day if I really wanted to.

I could blame him for my insecurities.
I could blame him for my perfectionism.
I could blame him for the parts of my body I'm not crazy about.
I could blame him for my struggles.

Hell, I could find things to blame him for that had little or nothing to do with him.

But none of that is true. None of that is REAL (not the kind of 'real' that I am committed to living at least). And it sure as hell would NOT serve my life and future versions of myself.

So one day I decided to stop blaming him, and I started taking ownership of my life. I started holding myself responsible for the things I had the power to change and the things I didn't love about my life.

And it wasn't until I started to see my life this way—to see that my dad (and no one else for that matter) had anything to do with the fact that my inner-Bitches were running my life --that I was able to:

★ Get to know their every move– where they show up, what they are saying to me, how they make me feel.
★ Disarm them and take away their weapons and insulting words (that I was taking personally).
★ Ditch them and become the one owning and influencing my life.

A Letter to My Younger Self

If I were zapping myself back in time to go help "Little Leanne" ward off the bitches, there's so much I would want to say to her.

The imaginary *Land of the Bitches* is all in good fun obviously, but the reality of it for me was that there was a lot of pain and struggle. Things were harder than they needed to be.

The *Bitches* I speak of are based on my life and my struggles from a very young age with confidence, self-esteem, weight loss, depression, and a number of other things.

I spent my whole life thinking they would go away when I lost the weight, but they didn't. Not even after I lost 100 lbs. and had the body I 'always wanted'. Not even close.

I wish I could have saved my younger self all the heartache and suffering I experienced growing up.

In fact, if I could send a note to "Little Leanne" before I left for my journey to the past to meet her, it would go something like this:

Dear Little Leanne,

Sweet beautiful, innocent, and perfectly imperfect Little Leanne.

There are going to be voices that will show up in your head and in your life. They might disguise themselves as your friends or pretend like they are doing you a favor or helping you. They may attempt to convince you that they can protect you by giving you the cold-hard truth, but do not be fooled into thinking they are your friends.

Oh no, my dear, they are your anti-BFF. They are the unsuspected haters in your life that will tear you down and pick you apart and talk you in and out of anything they feel like. They suck you in, chew you up, and spit you out without a second thought.

...They are the *Bitches*.

They are very sneaky and extremely good at what they do. Their one mission is to make you think you aren't:

- ★ Pretty enough
- ★ Skinny enough
- ★ Smart enough
- ★ Loveable enough
- ★ Successful enough.
- ★ Enough. Period.

And they'll do anything they can to keep you from feeling happy, believing in yourself, content, proud of yourself, or self-confident.

- ★ They'll bully you
- ★ They'll steal your smiles
- ★ They'll point out what goes wrong or what's missing
- ★ They'll spew venom to you about your body, your life, your significance, your responsibilities, and your value
- ★ They'll talk you out of going after what you *really* want, telling you things like "it's too dangerous" or "you don't deserve it" or "you'll never _____"
- ★ They'll try to control your every move and take over your inner-most thoughts.

DO NOT LET THEM.

Their presence is inevitable. Their perceived power is frightening. And their resilience is overwhelming. Even after you've kicked every last one out of your life, chances are, another will sneak in to fill her shoes, and it will most likely be when you least expect it.

It will feel like they out number you 10 to 1. You may feel powerless and weak and like no match for their numbing and debilitating words. But it's all an illusion my dear. None of it is real, yet all of can have a very real impact—if you let it.

I want you to always be on the lookout for these bitches. Not in a cautious or guarded way, just in a *"be aware"* kind of way.
Just like an umbrella allows you to still go live your life and do the things you want to do if you find yourself caught in the rain, this awareness will keep those bitches from completely ruining your day or 'calling in sick' to your life to avoid getting a little rain on you.

The last thing you have to watch out for: these bitches can be very sneaky—deceptive actually. They are masters of disguise. Oh, no. These bitches have a way of sneaking up on you, hijacking your own inner brain-workings, and making you believe it's actually YOU. Pay close attention to this special breed of *bitch*. They will hijack your mindset, but fortunately for you, they *do not* have access to your *brainset*. You do!

Right now, and every day from here on out, you are perfect just as you are, you are worthy of anything and everything that you desire, and only YOU can decide what that truly is. Your desires and your beliefs that you are worthy to obtain them are totally up to YOU! But it may not always seem that way when the bitches are around.

You are powerful beyond measure and can handle these meanies, no matter what!

Love,

Grown-up, Bitch-Smasher Leanne.

THAT is what I would tell her.

And I would also be sure to stress one really important thing about the bitches:

They will indeed show up whenever they feel like it, tell you to do X, Y, or Z, and boss you around like they own you, but you don't have to lay victim to their messages and methods when this happens.

When face-to-face with them, you have two choices:

1. You can let them boss you around and make your decisions **for** you.
2. You can *Ditch* them.

Accidental *Ditchery*

Looking back now, I can tell you exactly where my Bitches came from, what kept them coming back, and why their words hit home so deeply—why it always felt so personal.

But my younger self didn't know any of that. For the first 2/3 of my life I wasn't consciously choosing to live my life like I was powerless to my beliefs or all the reasons I thought I was 'fat' 'weird', or 'an embarrassment'. It's kind of just what happened. I didn't know that I had the power to change my own life at that point.

And of course, ditching them wasn't an option until it *was* an option.

I had to go out and figure it out first. Now I call it *Ditching*, but it started out simply as my reaction to my own life when I got so sick and tired of feeling bad about myself all the time.

My weight loss journey was the first monumental transformation of my life, and it was where the base-level of my foundation of Bitches started building.

I wasn't actively looking for them or actively trying to Ditch them though. I was simply doing whatever I needed to do to get away from a body that I hated and a lifestyle that I didn't feel in 'control' of.

My next transformation came when I had to literally learn to walk again after a back-debilitating injury and major spine surgery left my body feeling like anything but my own.

I was 25 at the time, but the truth is that I felt more like a 25-year-old trapped inside of an 80-year-old body.

I didn't have the language to describe it at the time, but my body just felt 'off'. The entire left side of my body (from pinky finger to pinky toe) lacked the same sensations that I had on my right side. And movements that I was once able to do with ease was now a complete 'blank' to my brain and the movement 'maps' of my body.

My doctor even told me I would probably "never be able to run again" and "should start looking into a career that didn't involve fitness". I mean just think about it: I had been 'weighing' and measuring my self-worth based on my body for as long as I could remember. I finally created the body I always wanted, and then POOF! It was suddenly "out of my control" in a completely new way. If I had listened to what my Body Bitches were telling me, I might still be sitting here feeling like my body was "broken".

And I won't get into all the details of my personal mindset and self-esteem transformation right this second. I'm talking I had ZERO confidence, ZERO self-esteem, and I was practically my own personal abusive boyfriend. But going to therapists to rehash the trauma I experienced when I lost my mom at the grocery store when I was 5, or if I still had underlying "daddy issues" did NOT help me learn how to love myself– to feel powerful and confident and beautiful to my bones.

But can you spot a common theme among all of these?

During my biggest struggles, I wasn't even aware that I was *Ditching Bitches* in the first place. I knew I was growing and evolving myself, and I knew I was trying to upgrade my self-esteem and confidence, but I wasn't acutely aware of what I needed to **eliminate** in addition to the things I wanted to add.

Can you imagine what would have happened if I did it all more intentionally though?

And as soon as I DID realize it—as soon as I became aware of these Bitches and created a system to live my life with intention and influence —my life started transforming faster than I ever thought possible. I mean talk about speeding up results fast!

That is when I knew I had to teach other women to do the same thing.

From Darkness to Light (Along A Path of Self-Love)

Before we get into the modern-day parable part of *Ditch the Bitch*, I'd like to share a few truths – from my heart to yours.

These are what I believe to be the (capital 'T') Truths about living in either 'darkness' or 'light'. The realities of remaining stuck in your current situation, or setting yourself free.

I believe we all have a darkness and a light that lives somewhere inside of us. For some women, the darkness never comes out, and the sky is always bright and sunshiny.

But for those that encountered a stormy day once upon a time and didn't learn how to let the sunshine come back in, chances are the darkness kept on coming back...and coming back... and coming back.

Unfortunately, that's the 'nature' of repeated darkness. It will keep coming back to the degree that you **practice** it – and the more you practice darkness, the more it peeks its way through.

For 30 years, I kept myself stuck. I fed my own darkness, telling myself the "ugly" stories. I was my own biggest internal-critic and my own biggest Bitch, and I downloaded a lot of things about myself that weren't true.

I worked my ass off figuring out solutions to the things that I THOUGHT were the reasons I felt so unhappy, but it didn't seem to help me.

I lost 100 pounds and ditched my overweight, out of shape lifestyle, but I still didn't FEEL beautiful.

I traveled, worked, and explored the globe, but it didn't help me find the FREEDOM I was looking for.

I created successful businesses, had more success, fortune and recognition than I knew what to do with, yet at the end of the day I was STILL miserable.

But here's why: Contrary to what I thought...

It wasn't my weight or my body that was making me unhappy.

It wasn't my geographic location or 'stagnant' life that was keeping me feeling stuck.

It wasn't a lack of things or stuff or jigamabobs keeping me from feeling fulfilled and truly happy.

It was ME.

More specifically it was the 'cast of characters' inside my mind that were calling all the shots in my life and impacting how I felt every single day. These voices are The Bitches that I speak of.

I know it may SEEM like if you just 'lose some weight', get a better job, or enter into a committed relationship (or whatever YOUR 'golden carrot' is) that suddenly all your troubles will magically disappear.

But take it from me. It does NOT work that way.

And for me, it didn't matter how 'skinny', adventurous, or 'wealthy' I became, my MINDSET and my HEADSPACE were still fat, in a prison of my own making, and damn poor!

A lifetime of "stinking thinking" doesn't just magically go away because you wish it away or lose a few pounds.

Here's what DID change things for me.

Getting to know my *Bitches* – seeing that they're not all bad and through learning to accept them –- that's how I've learned how to *Ditch* them.

Here's the other side of it though: Inner-Bitches will always be there; I believe it's part of being a human, and specifically, of being a woman.

But they don't have to run the show. And they don't have to keep you in the dark.

I discovered the skills to take me from my own version of *Bitcherella* to my own real-life *Ditcherella* (you'll see what I mean in a moment), and now it's **your** turn.

You see, when the darkness takes over, it tends to leave women feeling rather alone and a little hopeless for finding a solution. They're deflated and doubtful. It leaves them feeling STUCK. But this "stuckness" is created through a recipe of the Bitches' making.

And just as there is a recipe for Stuckness, there is a recipe for Freedom. It's the anti-nightmare. The dream. It's the fairytale of what life can be and IS when hope, belief, choice, action and flow are present. And it's a recipe I want every woman to create for herself.

So for the women of the world that did (for some reason or another) accidentally start practicing darkness, I want to show you how to practice something else. I want to teach you how to let the light back in.

And I want you to remind you again that:

It's never too late to go become who you really are.

It's never too late to go become the version of yourself you always wanted to become, but never knew was possible.

But the only way to truly find her is by travelling along a path of love (and often incorporating some forgiveness too).

It's a road of acceptance, connection, and care. It's a journey through know, like, and trust. And every woman deserves to know what life is like down this road.

No matter what you currently believe, for every woman who is a slave to her thoughts, feelings, and actions, the reality is that your 'enemy' is within.

But your enemy isn't REALLY your enemy. She's a scared little girl...or the parts of you that never grew up... or the voice inside of you SCREAMING at you to find a better way.

It's those voices of *The Bitches* that are keeping you feeling stuck and scared. And the voices will make sense when you learn to speak their language.

The things you want are MUCH closer than you think, but you won't get any closer if you don't change WHAT you think. And the story you tell yourself will only change when you decide that it MUST.

The Ditcherella Story (A Modern-Day Parable)

Once upon a time there lived a lovely woman named Ditcherella, who had a kind heart and big hopes and dreams.

But unfortunately she was caught between two worlds.

Her journey was the ultimate struggle between darkness and light --- perpetually caught between a life of happily ever after and unhappily never after.

Most of the time she was living, talking, and acting like her true self, Ditcherella. But sometimes she would get triggered and suddenly start seeing herself through the mind and eyes of her alter-ego, Bitcherella.

The battle within caused Ditcherella to struggle more than others, and oftentimes her struggling turned into suffering.

Bitcherella   **Ditcherella**

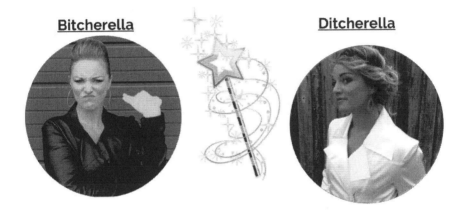

Her highs were really high, and her lows were REALLY low. And this struggle often left her feeling a little bit CRAZY, alone, and wondering if she was destined to be feel this way forever.

But then one day, Ditcherella's super-cool, ultra-wise Fairy Stepsister (from another mister) came along and helped her turn things around for good.

Her Stepsister's mission was to help her get off the up-and-down roller coaster of emotions, end the battle that was going on within, and get her started walking down a path that would make her feel happy and free. To show her a more EmPOWERing path to walk down; a path of EnLIGHTENment.

You see, her Fairy Stepsister wasn't trying to prevent Ditcherella's darkness from ever coming back, as she knew that darkness was an inevitability for any human being.

But she also knew that it was NOT the dark itself that was so crippling to Ditcherella...

It was her FEAR of the dark. It was what she knew, what she didn't know, and what she *didn't know she didn't know* that kept her SO stuck...and so AFRAID.

So Ditcherella's Fairy Stepsister simply wanted to help her make peace with the darkness, see that the darkness was a part of her (but didn't define her), and then teach her how to make her way back to the EnLIGHTENed path.

Her Fairy Stepsister was like the sister Ditcherella never had and the ultimate voice of truth and love.

Whenever Ditcherella became stuck in the mind of Bitcherella and couldn't find her own light, her Fairy Stepsister would appear like clockwork in her dreams and give her the light that she needed until she could find her power and make her way back towards the path of EnLIGHTENment.

All it took for her to go from STUCK to FREE was for her Fairy Stepsister (from another mister) to come along and essentially call her out on the belittling and untrue stories Bitcherella had started spinning inside her head (with love of course).

One day when Ditcherella was feeling especially defeated, her Fairy Stepsister appeared and said:

I don't mean to be the bearer of bad news, but can't you see that you are creating this stuckness, my sister? I say this with the upmost compassion, acceptance, connection, and care, but come on sister! I want to help you wake up!

You're beautiful and powerful and have extraordinary gifts inside of you-- even if sometimes it feels like the darkness is taking over. I assure you the beauty in your bones is way more powerful than ANY opposing force.

Right now you feel stuck and alone. And when you're stuck, it shrinks you. It fills you full of doubt, makes you feel lack, freezes you into inaction, and (in turn) causes even more stuckness. It pushes you further into the dark.

You're baking a recipe for Stuckness, one ingredient at a time. THAT is what's truly keeping you from the light.

But just like STUCK has a recipe my sister, so does FREEDOM.

That's why I am here: to tell you about the other recipe. You can use different ingredients as you travel along this journey, and they will take you down a different road. You will cross over a different bridge.

There is a recipe for Freedom. A recipe that takes you along the EnLIGHTENed path and keeps you travelling and growing as your TRUE self.

But you need to create yours one ingredient at a time...

I want you to think of who you are BEING when you're taking action. When you're believing in yourself and making choices you're proud of. When you're in your flow of life being easy and fun, and when you are happy! How does she think? How does she talk? How does she FEEL?

Who you're being when you're being THAT....take that and bottle that stuff up! That is YOUR recipe for freedom, one ingredient at a time. And there's no other recipe anywhere in the world quite like it.

But... if you keep using the same "Stuck" ingredients you're using now, you'll keep creating the same recipe. And it will keep leading you down the same road...forcing you to cross over the same bridge. And keeping you in the dark.

There are both real and imaginary gators inhabiting that water below. The more resilient and stable you are in your own internal bubble of love, acceptance, connection, and care, the easier it will be to find the other bridge – the bridge of Freedom - and the easier it will be to cross over.

But you can't run away from the darkness. And fighting it won't do you any good either.

Just let it be there. You can (and must!) learn to make peace with it. You must learn to be able to look at it in the eye. But for now, just let it be there.

It's allowed to scare you...and you don't have to like it. You can even wish it away if you desire.

But it does NOT define you! It is not WHO you are.

And you do have a choice. You DO have a choice as to whether or not you continue using those same ingredients, following that same recipe, and crossing over that same bridge.

I'm here to support you, care for you, and love you along the way. I can give you the ingredients and help you find your own recipe. But the ultimate choice is yours and yours alone to make. Which recipe do you want to cook up for yourself?

You have a choice, my dearest. Which version of yourself do you want to become? Who do you want to be and how do you want to feel? Which life do you want to lead?

See that there is a fork in the road right now, and you can continue in the dark along a path of Stuckness, or you can venture into Freedom. Into that life you've always dreamt of – full of beauty, happiness, and lightness.

Everything you need for either path already resides within you; you have the ingredients for both. The choice really is yours. Every single morning when you wake; the choice is yours. So which one do you choose today?

With love,

Your Stepsister (from another mister)

What's YOUR Story? *Bitchery* or *Ditchery*?

So this 'Face-Off' between darkness and light -- between your empowered self and your disempowered self -- like I said before, it will always be there.

It never fully goes away. From here on out, it simply becomes a matter of which one you 'feed'.

This short (other) parable shares my point perfectly:

"One evening an old Cherokee Indian told his grandson about a battle that goes on inside people. He said, 'My son, the battle is between two 'wolves' inside us all.

One is Evil. It is anger, envy, jealousy, sorrow, regret, greed, arrogance, self-pity, guilt, resentment, inferiority, lies, false pride, superiority, and ego.

The other is good. It is joy, peace, love, hope, serenity, humility, kindness, benevolence, empathy, generosity, truth, compassion and faith.'

The grandson thought about it for a minute and then asked his grandfather: 'Which wolf wins?'

The old Cherokee simply replied, 'The one you feed.'

Here's my point:

You can go learn any new 'way of being' if you decide it to be so -- if you choose it.

Because EVERYTHING is a skill.

We become good at whatever we practice -- whatever we give attention and repetition to.

And we can DEFINITELY place intentional focus and direction towards whatever it is that we want to become 'good' at.

For me it was no different.

- ★ I HATED how I felt about myself in my body.
- ★ I HATED how I felt about myself around food (before, during, and after I ate)
- ★ I HATED how I felt about myself on the inside -- how I treated myself with my words and my actions.

So I went out and intentionally changed those *ways of being* that I didn't approve of (and didn't want to accept from myself) any longer.

I intentionally practiced those changes until they became me -- until I **transformed**.

And I believe that YOU are no different.

Remember, I was about as far-gone and disconnected from my body (and self) as you could be: Crazy-addictive/controlling tendencies with food. Uber-critical and punishing relationship with my body. Outright abusive and loathing relationship with self.

So yea, I may seem like I see the world in rainbow-colored unicorns, but I truly believe that if I can do it, so can YOU!

But you have to make a choice once and for all.

Which one are YOU going to feed?

Your *Bitchery* story?

The one where you tell yourself that you are destined to stay STUCK forever? Where doubt and inaction and lack lead the way?

Or are you going to rewrite the story?

Are you going to create (and step into) your *Ditchery* story?

Your own story of finding self-acceptance and self-connection and self-love.

The one where you are the 'hero' in your own love story, and you save yourself from living a life of Bitchery.

But again, you DO have a choice.
Which one will you feed?

You don't have to know exactly what this looks like right now, but you simply have to decide to step into something NEW.

Or else you WILL keep 'feeding' the version of yourself that you know will keep you trapped in a cycle of pain, doubt, and more stuckness.

❤ You can CHOOSE (today!) to declare that you are finished with the beating yourself up, rejecting yourself, and giving yourself crap because you're not at a certain weight, bank balance, relationship status, or fill-in-the-blank.

❤ You can CHOOSE (today!) to end the 'war' you're in against yourself (and each of us have our own unique war that we waged once upon a time) and lay down the 'weapons' of shame and blame and comparison and perfectionism that are keeping you from living in the 'now' of your life — they keep you stuck in the past or fearful of the future, and they further lead to you REJECTING you.

❤ You can CHOOSE (today!) to make this DAY 1 of a kinder, loving, more compassionate approach to 'dealing' with yourself, to transforming your body, to anything really.

Because what's the alternative? And how long have you been trying out THAT alternative? And how is THAT working for you? I'd bet my money that it's NOT working for you.

You do have a choice. YOU are the ONE thing you can 'control'. But you have to CHOOSE it. You have to choose stepping into a newer version of yourself and a new way of being.

You DO have a choice. What will you choose?

Bitch Detecting Is Actually Easier Than Not

I used to carry my entire music collection around in one of those BIG CD cases. I never went anywhere without it. No road trip or vacation was complete without it for my music-fanatic self.

That is, until I got my first IPod. Now don't get me wrong, I know for the music collectors out there nothing compares to an unscathed 8 track or a book case full of CD's or albums, but for the sole purpose of listening to music in the most convenient, accessible, and efficient manner, there was no way I could go back to my old ways once I got wind of this magical little gadget called an iPod.

And yea, I knew I could have had 10 CD players for the price of that one iPod, but the time, energy, money, and sanity it would save me over the years, you couldn't have convinced me to do it the other way. And I'm pretty sure the rest of the world eventually came to that conclusion too.

If you had access to something that made your life easier-- that was essentially your key to cutting all those unnecessary and exhausting corners-- wouldn't you want to know about it too?

That is how I want you to start thinking about *Ditch the Bitch*.

If there was a "technology" or set of shortcuts that could make your life easier, more enjoyable, and enable you to eliminate all the B.S., the dead-ends, and exhaustion, wouldn't you want to at least know what it was.

Ditch the Bitch is essentially that "technology" that I built through my own personal experiences and my own little way of giving you the shortcut that I wish I had growing up. But the thing is: *Ditching Bitches* will actually take far less time and energy than NOT doing it.

Believe me, I wish I could say that I went and tried out all the dead-ends and failures on purpose because I was trying to "do you a solid" or "take one for the team", but that wouldn't be true.

It was because I didn't know of any better options. I didn't know what I didn't know...until I knew.

On top of that, I'm lazy in the same ways that all humans are lazy. I'd rather not waste a ton of time, energy, and resources on things that don't work, don't interest me, don't make my life better, or are simply unnecessary.

If there's a shortcut, and it doesn't get rid of the *experience* side of things that I might need to get, then I'd want to know about it! If something matters, and I really do need to go learn it by doing it, I'll work my ass off. But if there's an energy-saving "technology", I'd want to know about it. And I assumed you would too.

So are you ready for your new software upgrade? Are you ready to learn about what I deem to be the most potent superpower for getting yourself to actually do the things you WANT yourself to do and FEEL the way you want to feel? It's time for your upgrade and time to get your Bitch-Detection system installed. I assure you, it's going to change your life.

- → Results will come MUCH faster.
- → The journey will be easier and have MUCH less resistance.
- → You will start working on the solution instead of simply fixing the 'problem'.
- → And you will be completely transformed—not just temporarily changed.

You Can't Cheat the System

Thank g-d for science and research! Based on what we know about the brain and how your mind and body actually work--

from your mindset to your muscles -- we know that EVERYTHING is a skill. From juggling and playing soccer to weight loss and perfecting your lunges.

You wouldn't go buy your 16-year old teenager a brand new car, hand them the keys, and say "figure out how to drive it as you go honey, and be back in time for dinner!", right?

So why would you approach your transformation in that same manner?

Here's the thing though: you can't try to outsmart your brain.

Learning a new skill has a certain process. Remember our goal is to make your BEST YOU the new 'default' that you walk around with every day. Do 'the work' in the beginning, and then walk around with the skill the rest of your life (if you keep it fresh of course!). Here's the phases you MUST go through in order to get this new way of living to become the automatic, default way of living.

The Knowing: (This is the skill-set part of transformation)

When you first learn the basics of driving a car, you don't actually know yet how to drive a car and which handles do what. You might not even know what a car is. First you have to learn about your lack of knowledge and incompetence in this area, and then you can strive to learn about cars and how to actually operate them. Knowing what you *don't* know is just as important as knowing what you do know.

The Doing: (This is the hands-on practical application of the new skill)

Okay, so after you've learned what a car is, what knowledge you don't have in order to drive one, and learned about those missing pieces, then you can actually start trying it out and putting all that information to use. Then you can learn how to operate a car and discover what handles do what as you are *actively learning* how to drive. You must however focus a lot on the task or else you'll make mistakes. This first part of learning a new skill has to be *conscious* and *cognitive*. You've got to be actively paying attention to the task at hand. Remember: learning about something doesn't give you the physical and practical ability to successfully do it.

The Living (Experiencing): (This is the part where you are actually using the new skills as it fits into YOUR real life.)

Once you have gotten your driver's license and you've been driving for a while, driving is easy. You don't need to concentrate as hard as you once did, and you (kind of) go on auto-pilot. You have the capacity to relax, turn up the radio, and even talk on the phone (well maybe that's not the best idea).

But you can easily wrap your head around the fact that the more driving you do, the better driver you become. And the better you become, the less you have to consciously think about it every time you do it.

Unfortunately most people don't understand that this is how it works for anything you want to be good at, and it's the part that most people SKIP altogether.

- ★ It's the practicing tuba to get good at tuba part
- ★ It's the speaking Spanish to get better at speaking Spanish part
- ★ It's the 'work' and 'hard yards' that you need to put in to make whatever it is you want as automatic as brushing your teeth.

It's the part NOT to be skipped over.

Ditchery Is a Skill

Would you sit down in a classroom in the morning to learn a new language, and leave in the afternoon fluent in the 'mother tongue'?

Would you pick up a new musical instrument one day and go to bed with Beethoven's confidence and Simon Cowell knocking down your door?

Would you send your kid to the first day of kindergarten and expect them to know college algebra by the time the afternoon bell rings?

And would you walk up to a man or women that intrigues you that you'd only just met and ask them if they'd like to make crazy hot love to you and marry you right then and there?

Skills need consistent practice, commitment, care, and the courage to continue going even if you mess up or get frustrated or (gulp!) completely SUCK at it at first.

Relationships need consistent practice, commitment, care, and the courage to keep on going even if they get messy up or frustrating.

Happiness is a skill, a relationship and a commitment just like powering through the first few weeks of playing guitar when your fingers feel like burning, worn-out nubs.

Creating the body that reflects who you REALLY are is a skill and a relationship and a commitment just like love when it hits the rocks and you get beaten and battered and tossed in the wind.

Confidence and courage– yep you guessed it. They are skills and relationships and commitments– and ones that you don't HAVE to have. You *could* go on living and breathing just fine if you never had them.

So why would you look at any skill or relationship–the ones that need practice and study and time and care– and expect to be a master in one day? To just have them and keep them and not have to give them another thought ever again?

Or to earn someone's trust in a minute or a day and expect it to just always be there without another thought and without another care?

Confidence, owning your beauty, courage, and transformation. They are all a skill, all a practice, and all of them happen to be right there waiting for you to grab.

But you've got to learn the skills.

You've got to practice consistently.

And you've got to 'water them' and care for them and pay tribute to them, or else they might not stick around.

Ditchery Is a *Practice*

I learned from my days in health and fitness industry that "losing weight" and "having a body that you love and are proud of" are two VERY different things.

If you walk up to a typical woman and ask her what she thinks about her body– what she sees and feels when she looks in the mirror– the majority tell you what she DOESN'T like about her body.

* ★ Where she's got excess fat or 'squishy-ness' than she would like to get rid of
* ★ Where her stomach hangs over her pants and creates a 'muffin top' or 'love handles'
* ★ Where her thighs pucker and cellulite tends to accumulate
* ★ Where there's excess fat flying around in the back of her arms every time she waves hello
* ★ Where there's wrinkles or brow lines that keep getting darker with age
* ★ Where her hair isn't straight enough, where here toe nail polish isn't perfect enough, how her jeans aren't small enough...

You get the picture.

Now I'm not going to try and make up some random statistic just to shock you or send your jaw to the ground. (83.2% of statistics are actually made up anyways) ☺

But I'm going to throw out a number that is based on my everyday interactions with dealing with THIS SPECIFICALLY: How women **feel** about their bodies.

This number is based on hundreds of individuals, thousands of hours, and countless conversations about the [perceived] shape, tone, texture, and beauty a woman's body.

I'm going to venture to say that 95% of the women that I talk to DON'T FEEL BEAUTIFUL. They don't love their bodies, appreciate their curves, embrace their imperfections, or like what they see when they look in the mirror.

No matter how much they work out, how little they eat, or how much progress they make, when they look in the mirror, their eyes and mind flock to all the things they DON'T like about their bodies, and focus on what they DON'T want-- what they might even go as far to say they HATE or makes them DEPRESSED.

Yep. These findings have been predictable and consistent: How a woman FEELS about her body has little or nothing to do with her ACTUAL body.

- ★ I've seen women get super-lean, super-fit, and super-toned and still HATE what they see in the mirror.
- ★ I've seen women agonize and obsess over the number on the scale, only to still HATE the reflection they see in the mirror– even after they hit their goal weight.
- ★ I've seen women completely makeover their bodies from head to toe– changing their shape, body composition, the way they walk and move and still feel like nothing has changed– like their bodies didn't change one bit.

But you know what else I've seen?

I've seen women (who without changing a single physical thing or feature) have improved their confidence in a matter of minutes.

I've seen women GAIN weight, but also fall in love with themselves or another person at the same time, and improve their confidence and sense of self very quickly.

I've seen women get STRONGER, FITTER, LEANER, and TIGHTER (without necessarily losing a bunch of weight) do the same thing: improve how they feel about what they see and how they feel.

I truly believe that feeling BEAUTIFUL and CONFIDENT and POWERFUL has much less to do with how you look than you think.

But if it's not just about the body, what is it about?

I am going to share a belief that some might think to be crazy. Others might think it's impossible. And others might just think it applies to everyone else BUT them.

But not only do I believe this wholeheartedly based on my experiences and interactions with myself and 100's of other women– but I also believe this based on what I've obsessively studied and now know about neuroscience, the brain, perceived threat, and human behavior and psychology:

Loving your body (and loving yourself) — feeling LOVEABLE and BEAUTIFUL and CONFIDENT– each one is a set of SKILLS. Each one is a PRACTICE.

Wanna feel beautiful? Learn the SKILLS and commit to the PRACTICE of feeling beautiful.

Wanna feel confident? Learn the SKILLS and commit to the PRACTICE of feeling confident.

Wanna LOVE yourself completely, fully, and without exception? Yep, it's a practice too... and you need the skills to back it up.

What I'm saying is this:

Just like learning a new language, a new sport, how to ride a bike or read. Living in a body and a life that makes you feel beautiful confident, and proud is a skill set-- one that anybody can learn.

The same goes for any and every area of your life. Everything is a skill.

Ditchery Has Its Own Equation

Ever catch an episode of the show 'Hoarders'? The one where they go into people's homes that look like they have never been de-cluttered or organized, and contain SO much stuff– so much that they can barely even see the floor?

Imagine that you had a garage like that and you needed to get things organized and decluttered. Where would you begin? It's a madhouse inside that overstuffed garage, and certainly you have to have some sort of strategy for tackling this beast right?

Let's look at a couple different options:

Option 1: You decide to do it in chunks. You divide the garage into four corners, and you start to go at it one corner at a time.

What happens? You end up having an organized version of the mess that was once there. You never truly have the ability to get an aerial view of what you have and what you don't have— you never had the ability to IDENTIFY everything. You could come across the backup copy of "Green Eggs and Ham" that you bought after you misplaced the first copy, but you'd have to decide whether to keep it or give it away without being able to know if the other part of the garage contains the other copy. Not to mention, this garage is so filled with so much junk and trash, that you wouldn't even know if there was a dead cat in there somewhere! It's like going in there blind. You can't take a proper inventory or get an idea of where things should go (let alone what you actually want to go anywhere).

Option 2: Remove EVERYTHING from the garage completely first—not a single item remaining– and go from there.

What happens? Now you have breathing room– a little altitude and distance. You're not so overwhelmed by everything that's lying around, and you can actually RESPOND to the situation at hand, rather than REACT. Now you can organize everything at once OUTSIDE of the garage. First, you would simply go through and start tossing all the things you KNOW you don't want.

★ A single flip-flop here.
★ A dog collar for your dog that is no longer around.
★ All of those old clothes that don't fit you anymore, you haven't worn in 3 years, and don't ever plan of wearing again.

You get the picture. Going through the clutter and throwing away the trash or the stuff that you OBVIOUSLY don't want any more is the easy part. You know what you DON'T want– the blatantly obvious stuff.

Now that all of that stuff is out of the way, you can actually start creating a bit of order. You've got your 'throw away' pile, your 'give away' pile, and of course the pile of stuff you want to put back in and keep. THEN (and only then) can you actually see what else you might need to buy if you find you do need something. And then you can proceed to put the items back in the garage in an organized fashion. Now you can feel relaxed, uncluttered, and actually have method to the madness. And talk about setting yourself up for RESPONDING in the future (vs. REACTING).

Looking for your tire pump? Easy, it's got a space on a shelf. It takes you 1/3 of the time that it would take in your old garage simply locating that ol' thing. Looking for bungee cords to attach that now-inflated bike to your bike rack? No problem, you don't have to spend the time (and energy) scouring the grounds for them.

See how it works?

But you couldn't get to that point if you didn't first get rid of all the things that you KNOW you don't want– all the things that aren't serving you by keeping around anyways.

And if you think about it, that's the best way to go and figure out what you do want in your own life!

Now think about your own life. Where are you constantly trying to organize your current overwhelm, keep up with your growing list of to-do's, and add in new things to the never-ending pile? Where have your current life and your current list of goals, wants, and desired, become an over-stuffed, hoarded garage?

In other words, are you too mentally cluttered to go out and get what you really want?

Think about it: Figuring out what you do want is one of the more challenging parts of transformation. You might feel confused, not have enough information, or feel overwhelmed by options. But recognizing and identifying what you don't want is the easy part!

★ How do you NOT want to feel?
★ What do you want to eliminate in your life?
★ What foods do you know you should eliminate to feel and look your best?
★ What people should you eliminate contact with because they don't promote you becoming a better version of yourself?
★ Where do you NOT want to go?
★ What things or activities do you want to STOP doing?
★ What habits do you need to stop?

So let the 'what do I want' part just be for little a bit, and instead focus on eliminating what you DON'T want.

Remember, before you start buying new stuff or organizing a cluttered closet or garage, give yourself some space and breathing room by eliminating the stuff that you know isn't working for you....and give yourself somewhere to get started while you focus on figuring out what you do want.

Start with the 'not' questions. Start by SUBTRACTING– not ADDING more.

And THAT is exactly why ditching the bitches in your life has to be the first step of your transformation. Otherwise you would be throwing a bunch of new habits and beliefs into a clutter-filled mess of thoughts and beliefs. The new ones wouldn't have a chance in hell.

Living Groundhog's Day

It's really important to define the most important aspects of designing a life that you love, what it would take to get you there, and what you ARE and are NOT willing to do to get there.

You want to feel POWERFUL & like the sole INFLUENCE in the process, right? We know what happens when the process confines you or takes over your life—or even worse: when you actually HATE it. So it's important to find that happy medium between results and your experience of life so that you can stay the course.

If you've been around the transformation 'block' a time or two, and probably just as fed up with cookie-cutter approaches that just feel wrong to you as I am. Those ones that don't fit in your lifestyle or a way of living that you could possibly sustain.

The truth is: if YOU still don't know what the best plan is for you and your ideal life, then NO ONE does. It's time to approach your goals like the 'mad scientist' that you are deep down inside and go create a WINNING game plan that was actually designed for YOU.

And that's why I encourage you to use the principles and tools in this book to go craft your own personal 'Mad' Science Experiments.

Imagine using your past experiences – success and failures – as nothing more than mere DATA about what works and doesn't work for your life, what you do and don't like or want incorporated in your plan of action, and what types of situations set you up to SUCCEED.

Then imagine taking that information and setting you up so that you can actually ENJOY your experience of life while you are working hard towards whatever it is that you want.

We already talked about the fact that if 'results' are all you are seeking, then that's all you're going to get, right?

I saw this happening all the time in the fitness and weight loss industry, so I decided to dig a little deeper.

I asked my clients if they would join a program and work their ass off if they knew they would end up right back where they started not too long down the road. If they knew it was going to be a failure (or that they would regress right away), would they invest their time, energy, and resources in the first place?

And I got an overwhelming amount of "HELL NO's!"

How many times have you "gone on a diet" in your life? Or *tried* to quit X, Y, or Z? Or start X, Y, or Z?

How many times have you tried to make changes to your life or tried to do anything?

If you added up the time, money, energy, and frustrations you've spent on trying things-- only to try them again down the road, and then try them AGAIN down the road, you would be shocked.

How many 1000's of dollars and hours have you spent on certain things in your life– buying anything and everything that would help you 'make changes'?

So what's up with those changes now? Did you conquer them? Did you beat them?

It all comes back to making sure you are playing a 'Winning Game' —one that you can get the results you are looking for while still enjoying the EXPERIENCE of your life.

Transforming your body, evolving your career, increasing your confidence, becoming a more organized person —none of it can happen if you can't even stick to the plan, right?

So if you were a "HELL NO" in response to the question above, I encourage you to ask yourself how you can do things right, and do them for good– so you can go spend your time, energy, and money on whatever you want to spend it on.

Your Super Power: Awareness

Looking back I can now see that the periods in my life that I (did and still do) feel majorly unhappy or defeated or feel like pulling the covers back over my head and hiding from the world, it's usually because there is a *Bitch* is in the driver's seat of my mind.

And just to clear things up here from the beginning, this is not a past-tense thing either. I still struggle every single day to make sure I'm the one running my life.

Yep, I too fall victim to my own Bitches. And I wasn't able to start influencing it until I became AWARE of it.

So I'm sure you're wondering: Okay already, let's get on with this! Tell me how to ZAP these meanies and put the bitches in their place? I can only imagine you might be ready to cut to the chase.

Before we can tame these ladies and put them on some tight leashes, we have to uncover a very important piece of the puzzle first:

You have to know what you are looking for!

What good would it do if you were equipped with the tools to be a *Bitch-Ditching* Ninja if you were essentially clueless to realize when the bitches were actually in the room with you?

How can you seek out what you don't know how to look for?

And that's why it's the first step and oh-so-critical to hone in your own bitch-detecting skills first and foremost.

I urge you to start searching for them: to start actively seeking them out in your life, and (ideally) just let them be there. And when your internal ninja wants to scream and fight and tell those bitches off, resist the urge!

Instead let yourself see them showing up without judgment and without shame and just create a little checkmark in your mind.

That's a bitch right there. That's another bitch right there.

If you can simply get really good at identifying them and labeling them as such, you'll never feel powerless to the bitches in your life again. But more on that in just a bit.

Why You Want To Speak Fluent 'Bitch'

Imagine if your best friend walked up to you and said:

> *"Whoa! Do not leave the house wearing THAT! Your hair makes your face look ugly...that outfit is sooo 2011, and no one will ever give you the time of day because of those thick thighs of yours! You're fat. You're not very bright. You're kinda just... Bleh!"*

You think you'd be hanging out with that BFF of yours much longer? Yeah, probably not.

But when you think about it, that's how the large majority of women talk to themselves. Maybe not all the time, but enough of the time for it to matter and make a difference in how we see ourselves. And because it's so common, we often fail to see that it's even happening—that it's actually a case of the bitches showing up and setting up shop in your own lives.

When you ask yourself a question, does your answer sound like you are talking to someone you love? Or does it sound more like one of the *bitches* in your life is answering?

It's crucial for you to start paying attention to the language you are using to talk to yourself every day, and start standing for yourself like you would if someone ELSE used those words against you.

Just imagine how you would feel if someone else spoke to you that way. It's time to start standing for yourself – as in **raising**

your standards and what you choose to accept into your life. You deserve it!

But I don't mean to FIGHT your bitches. I don't mean to get aggressive, mad, mean, or resist them.

Basically it's a matter of getting really good at knowing when a certain bitch shows up, and practicing just letting her be there. Don't try and tell her to *bugger off*. Don't try to get out your brass knuckles and duke it out. Just become aware.

Essentially you want to start becoming super AWARE of when you detect Bitch-speak in your mind. And the only way to do that is to start becoming hyper-aware of the words you are using to describe yourself and your life.

What are you saying to yourself? What are you saying about yourself? Bring that to your CONSCIOUS mind starting right now. Then, we can talk about raising the bar on your own standards of how you choose to be treated — by others, but especially by yourself.

It's a matter of seeing what you aren't seeing, noticing what you aren't noticing, and becoming aware of how you are talking TO yourself and ABOUT yourself.

RANDOM RAMBLES FROM LEANNE:

Language can be such a weird thing. I didn't realize how many words I was misusing until I started actually thinking about what I was saying....and I started looking up the etymology and meanings of words. (Yes I'm a big geek).

For example, the word *success* actually means "happy outcome" or "accomplishment of desired end".

Why is it that oftentimes once we (myself included) get what we think we want, it doesn't leave us feeling happy for very long, and it's often NOT our desired end? We usually end up thinking about the NEXT thing... and the NEXT thing... and rarely take time to bask in that 'thing' we just worked our asses off for?

Double dog dare: Whatever it is you think you want to 'be' or 'become' in your life -- whether it's successful, rich, happy, confident, loved, fill-in-the-blank -- go look up the ACTUAL definition of the word and see what it *really* means and how you've been using it.

And you might just find that you already are that 'thing'....and have been that thing all along.

For me I realized this usually happens when I spend my energy focusing on the RESULT itself and not my EXPERIENCE of life while seeking the result, or how I want to FEEL at the end of it.

Something You MUST Understand

Imagine for a second that you don't know how to tie your shoe. Tying your shoe is an actual skill that you need to initially be taught (and then continue practicing) so that you get better at it right?

Then after a while (with enough practice), it would become automatic in your brain. You wouldn't need logic or reason or consciously think about tying the laces in order to do it successfully. After a while you would sort of start to tie your shoe on autopilot.

Now imagine trying to learn how to tie a shoe for the very first time, but while you are sitting outside attempting it, you see a massive funnel cloud appear overhead and all of a sudden a tornado is right down the street from where you are sitting.

Do you think your brain will allow you to access the thoughts and logic you need to **learn** to tie your shoe, or do you think it will start focusing on getting you out of harm's way?

There's a major paradox that exists when it comes to learning the skills that will enable you to *Ditch the Bitch* whenever one shows up. It might sound a bit counter-intuitive, but in order to actually learn these skills, you must be **away** from the Bitches. They **cannot** be around while you are acquiring these skills—just like a tornado **cannot** be around if you want to learn how to tie a shoe (or learn any other new skill).

That's because *Bitchery* and *Ditchery* live in two different parts of your brain.

Sounds a little strange right?

I mean if you want to feel confident that you have what it takes to overcome your Bitches, wouldn't it make sense that you have to do it while they are actually there in front of you?

I can see why this might confuse you. Allow me to explain.

Ditchery is not just something that automatically takes place if you simply know that *Bitches'* wrath are upon you. Knowing that they are there is important, but it's not enough to actually disarm them.

Ditchery is a skill that can be practiced and improved indefinitely over time, but you cannot (as in, your brain won't let you) to access the power you need to learn those skills while the Bitches are around.

You'll learn more about this later, but it's really important to understand that the human brain's job is to detect **threat** and **danger**. It uses things like pain or your perception or gut feeling that something is bad to happen as its warning system.

It's important to know that **the *Bitches* ARE a threat** (OR they are what cause your brain to get into a threatened state), and your brain is very aware of this fact when they show up.

Related Geekery

Getting into a bit of "Geekery" for a moment, it's important to note that the part of the brain that experiences threat and danger and does whatever it needs to do to make us feel 'safe', is a segment of our brain all on its own. It's the reptilian part of our brain.

The logic and reason we need to use to see that the *Bitches* are saying things that might not be true or might be based on our own perceptions, is a separate segment of the brain altogether. This happens in the human part of our brain.

But essentially, those two separate parts of the brain WILL NOT 'turn on' at the same time. There's plenty of "Geekery" beyond the scope of this book to elaborate, but for purposes of your *Bitches*, just know that when they are around and they are stirring up your emotions, you will not be able to logic or reason or "positive think" your way to a better mindset.

You won't be able to access that part of your brain. Your nervous system won't let you. It's busy "putting out the fire" in the *other* part of your brain.

And no offense, but if your brain detects danger, it's going to be more concerned with getting you **out** of danger than it is with making sure that you feel warm and fuzzy while doing so.

So what does this mean for your *Bitch-Detecting* journey? Well this is actually very useful *intel.*

Often times we feel weak or powerless to remind ourselves of the reality of the situation while we are in it. When we can't flip that switch and "put on a happy face", it's easy to think there's something 'wrong' with us.

But now that you know that it has nothing to do with your mindset — that it's in fact your *brainset* that is responsible for this task— you can cut yourself a bit of slack.
You aren't "weak" or "powerless" or a "failure" when you feel powerless against the Bitches. Your brain is actually forcing you to face the more imminent *danger* and forcing you to seek *safety*—whatever or wherever it deems that to be.

Imagine your brain with a line drawn right down the middle to split it into two sections. (This isn't a direct representation of the actual segmentation in your brain, but I just want you to be able to actually picture in your head the concept that *Bitchery* and *Ditchery* live in two different parts of the brain).

Ditchery   **Bitchery**

LOGIC   THREAT!

REASON   DANGER!

LEARN NEW SKILL   RUN!

Oftentimes we blame ourselves as the reason that something didn't work out the way we wanted it to. Other times we simply blame ourselves for the way we are (or aren't) feeling.

We might think it's because we are 'weak' or 'powerless' or 'out of control' or 'not worthy' or 'not good enough'. Whatever it is that we say or don't say, oftentimes we choose to take it personally—like there's some fatal flaw within US.
Especially if it's something that we know is possible—that we've seen someone else do with ease 1000 times-- surely it must be us then right?

But now that you know what you know about the brain and how the actions that you want to take can only be possible if your brain feels safe, doesn't it feel a lot less personal?

Here's what you need to know in order to become your own personal mean, lean, Bitch-Ditching machine!

1. *Ditchery* is a skill. It's a 'way of being' that you can practice (and get better and better at) where you become the version of yourself where your Bitches don't impact you or influence you as much (and eventually you influence THEM even more). Just like learning to ride a bike or speak a new language, you need your 'logic and reason' and skill-learning brain in order to acquire (and get good at) this skill.

2. When your Bitches are around, you are under threat. The Fight/Flight/Freeze part of your brain will have no choice but to be activated, and its main priority will be getting you of threat.

3. Therefore, you cannot access the part of the brain that you need in order to learn the skills of *Ditchery* – not while the Bitches are around. Your brain will not let you.

4. You need to make your brain feel 'safe' in order for it to focus on *Ditchery* skills.

Part 2: UNDERSTANDING THE LANGUAGE OF THE BITCH

Detoxing From Your Bitches (The Truth About Your Self-Talk)

If you want to take back your power and break UP with that version of you that is judging you, nitpicking, and keeping you stuck....

And if you want to break OUT of that disempowering relationship with yourself and go earn back your own trust and respect....

We need to first elevate your THINKING

Because in order to BE your most empowered self, you have to practice becoming your empowered self. Thinking like her, talking like her, feeling like her.

You can go get empowered temporarily from someone (or something) else, but if you want to have it, you have to cultivate that ability within yourself.

You need to actively feed yourself with 'Freedom Thinking' (just like Ditcherella needed to do), and I know from my own personal experiences that it truly IS an 'inside job'.

So how do you do that? Simple!

You must start with a lil' *Awareness Awareness.* Basically it's a matter of 'tuning in' to your own inner-voice and seeing where your Self-Talk and BodyTalk has been taken over by YOUR Bitches and (essentially) become *Bitch-Talk* instead.

And of course you need to do a little 'makeover' on it, so that the REAL you is the one calling the shots.

So what is *Awareness Awareness*?

You don't know what you don't know, right? How can you see what you aren't looking for?

So *Awareness Awareness* is a matter of noticing what you're not noticing, seeing what you're not seeing, and feeling what you're not feeling.

Essentially all you need to do is start paying attention! You need to simply become mindful of how you are talking **to** yourself **about** yourself, how you are treating yourself, and what you are **saying** and **seeing** when you look in (both the real and the metaphorical) mirror.

The awareness of your Self-Talk and BodyTalk is one part of it. A lot of women aren't even aware of this awareness though – that it's a skill you can learn and cultivate. So that that you're aware of this awareness, THAT is an *Awareness Awareness*. ☺

If you simply become aware of your current BodyTalk and Self-Talk, see where YOUR Bitch-Talk is showing up, and create some (other) new *Awareness Awarenesses*, things will start to shift for you. VERY quickly.

Awareness Awareness of what exactly you might be wondering?

Allow me to shed some light on what's REALLY keeping you stuck.

The 5 Bitchery *Awareness Awarenesses*:

1. **Guilt:** Feeling bad about what you are or are not **DO**ing. (literally means: crime, sin, fault, fine, moral defect or failure of duty)
2. **Shame:** Feeling bad about who you are or aren't **BE**ing (literally means: loss of esteem or reputation, to cover, feeling disgrace)
3. **Blame:** Placing responsibility on someone else, something else, or yourself. (literally means: condemn, find fault, criticize)
4. **Comparison:** Using black/white language like 'good', 'bad', 'right', 'wrong', 'healthy', 'unhealthy', or 'should', 'shouldn't', 'are supposed to', 'are not supposed to', 'allowed, 'not allowed'. But also... comparing yourself to others, to where you used to be, or to where you think you're 'supposed to' be. (literally means: Liken, rival)
5. **Perfectionism:** Nothing is ever enough. Good enough, fast enough, done enough, successful enough. Enough PERIOD. (literally means: to bring to full development)

Looking Out For 'Faulty Math'

'Faulty Math' is the difference between what ACTUALLY happened....vs what YOU SAY about what happened.

In other words, it's the DATA of the situation...vs. the DRAMA that you added to it.

Here's some examples:

GUILT STORIES:

★ **What ACTUALLY Happened (The DATA):** You ate a cupcake.

★ **Guilt DRAMA:** *"I ate that cupcake. I wish I hadn't done that/ eaten that. That was 'bad'. That was 'wrong'."*

★ **Again, The DATA:** You ate a cupcake.

The math doesn't add up!

★ **The TRUTH**: Guilt zaps the fun out of the here and now. If your inner rule enforcer is always chiming in about the 'right' or 'wrong' way to do something, what's 'good' or 'bad', or what you 'should, would, or could' be doing (this is all in comparison to the status quo or your idea of perfection of course), you're never going to get to actually enjoy the experience of your life.

SHAME STORIES:

★ **What ACTUALLY Happened (The DATA):** You ate a cupcake.

★ **Shame DRAMA**: *"I ate that cupcake. Therefore I am a [fatass/weak-willed/ unmotivated/a self-sabotager/fill-in-the-blank]. I am 'bad'. I am 'wrong'. "*

★ **Again, The DATA:** You ate a cupcake.

The math doesn't add up!

★ **The TRUTH:** Eating that cupcake does not mean that you are 'weak-willed' or a 'self-sabotager'. In fact nothing about what you do or don't do has to mean anything about who you are as a person. I'm not telling you that you need to love all of your decisions or actions, but you don't need to apologize for who you are either. You also don't need to apologize for how you feel, and you certainly don't need to apologize for your past, hide yourself, disgrace yourself, or shame yourself for what you did or didn't do.

BLAME STORIES:

★ **What ACTUALLY Happened (The DATA):** You ate a cupcake.

★ **Blame DRAMA:** "I ate that cupcake. It's all [my fault/my husband's fault/the cupcake's fault! There needs to be 'consequences'!"]

★ **Again, The DATA:** You ate a cupcake.

The math doesn't add up!

★ **The TRUTH:** The only way to truly own your life is to take responsibility for it. Sometimes things happen and there is no logical explanation, and it doesn't need to be anyone's fault. Finger-pointing and blaming doesn't take away from what happened or change the facts. In fact it keeps you living in the past by dwelling. And most often (especially if you have your Inner-Bitch on your shoulder) the finger usually gets pointed right back at yourself.

COMPARISON STORIES

★ **What ACTUALLY Happened (The DATA):** You ate a cupcake.

★ **Comparison DRAMA**: *"I ate that cupcake. Last week I was doing so 'good', now I'm doing 'bad'...* or *"Other women don't act like this around cupcakes! What's wrong with ME?"*

★ **Again, The DATA:** You ate a cupcake.

The math doesn't add up!

★ **The TRUTH:** Comparison can be a valuable tool. It can help us create distinctions in our mind, figure out our own preferences, and generally help us detect apples from oranges. Comparison can also be used as a weapon to judge, shame, and critique ourselves (and others). Comparison to what you shoulda, woulda, or coulda done...or where you should be, would be, or could be.

Here's the truth: You are never going to be just like anyone else. You're a snowflake (cheesy as it may sound), and that will never change. But if you continue to liken and compare yourself to others and it's not serving you, that's a mindset shift that you have the ability to make right away. The human brain is designed to spot patterns and create associations, but if those associations are making you feel less than, that's on you, and you don't have to keep doing it.

PERFECTIONISM (CONTROL) STORIES:

★ **What ACTUALLY Happened (The DATA):** You ate a cupcake.

★ **Perfectionism DRAMA:** *"I ate that cupcake. Now I've ruined my diet. I was being perfect all week, and that cupcake just ruined it!. Game over. Time of Death? Call it a 'failure'."*

★ **Again, The DATA:** You ate a cupcake.

The math doesn't add up!

★ **The TRUTH:** Call it what you want: Perfectionism, control, micro-managing. If it serves you, that's great. Truth is I've yet to meet a woman that doesn't drive herself crazy over it.

I refer to control as a 'losing game'. It's perfectly natural to desire that certain things happen in a certain way, but when we create requirements that everything happens according to plan (requirements to be happy, to feel successful, to feel good about ourselves), that's when it backfires. And it's only because we will never truly be able to control every**thing** and every**one** in our lives. It's an impossibility. But we do have the power to influence ourselves and our lives to our greatest abilities.

Happiness stems from freedom, not control. But we can only feel truly free when we have the ability to choose. Restrictions and control are the polar opposite of freedom.

A Note About Our Stories

If any of the above stories resonated with you, put a smile on your face, or made you want to raise your hand and say "yep that's, me!"...

That's a GREAT thing.

Yes I used a cupcake as an example, but the lesson and the metaphors come across no matter what's at stake or what 'lens' you are looking at yourself through.

We all have our own breed of Bitches roaming around, infiltrating our mindset, and telling their own version of the Truth (with a Capital 'T').

The goal is to own that fact, and go influence them MORE than they influence us. And the simplest way to do that is:

- ★ Accept them and get to know them.
- ★ Understand them.
- ★ Go influence YOU. Who you're being, what you're doing, and how you're feeling.

In other words:

- ★ Know thy Bitches
- ★ Understand thy Bitches
- ★ Ditch (Influence) thy Bitches

Let's continue, shall we? ☺

Bitches Aren't All Bad

Imagine you had a big chunk of blueberry in your teeth from your morning smoothie. A not-so-nice person might laugh or point or try to make you feel stupid about it. A kind and considerate person might pull you aside and tell you discretely that you have a 'lil something' in your teeth.

Regardless of how the news is broken to you, at the end of the day, you still had a blueberry stuck in your teeth. That's information that most people would want to know, right?

That's kind of how the Bitches are.

You see the tricky thing about your Bitches (and your current Self-Talk and Bodytalk) is that it isn't **all** bad.

Okay so maybe you didn't need to feel humiliated about the blueberry that got stuck, and even though it wasn't handled in the nicest way, there was STILL a blueberry there.

So I want you to start thinking about how you can use the Bitchery you encounter and witness to your advantage... to find out the truth of how you *really* feel about yourself, your life, your situations.

In this case, the truth shall set you free! But it's also VERY helpful *recon* moving forward.

Kind of like your own weather forecast for a major hurricane.

You just got word that a category 3 hurricane is headed right for you, and you've got about 72 hours to prepare for its arrival.

Okay, that sounds like pretty bad news. But *how bad* is it?

You feel threatened, you feel vulnerable, and maybe even downright fearful of the dangers of the storm. But wouldn't you be even *more* threatened and *more* vulnerable if you *didn't* know about the impending disaster? And couldn't the outcome, in fact, be worse?

The Bitches in your life are no different.
The cold-hard truth: They (your Inner-Bitches) will always be there. No matter how strong and resilient and powerful you feel or become. No matter how much personal development

and personal growth "work" you do on yourself. No matter how bitch-proof you strive to become. The question is:

★ How well can you detect them?
★ How well can you understand them, and use what you're 'hearing' to your advantage?
★ How well are you influencing YOU? Who you're **be**ing, what you're **do**ing, and how you're **feel**ing moment-by-moment, day-to-day. (It's the only thing in your life you can 'control'!)

And how can you go about doing all of that 'Ditching'...in a loving and peaceful and as stress-less-as-possible way?

Without all of the 'weight' that you're currently carrying around:

★ The weight of the shame, blame, guilt, comparison, and perfectionism that's permeated your inner-chatter.
★ The weight of any stress, worry, or burden you may be carrying around.
★ The weight of any physical, mental, social, or emotional pain or dis-ease (*brain pain*).
★ The wait. Waiting to **be** who you want to be, **do** what you want to do, and **feel** how you want to feel until you've 'arrived' – whether it's a number on a scale, a bank balance, or a relationship status. Anything (that's outside of you) that's keeping you from feeling like you're LIVING your life to its fullest extent or possibility.

But if you commit to getting to know the bitches in your life and start learning to predict and respond to how you're currently reacting to them, you're going to eventually feel like a Master Meteorologist when there's an impending *Bitchstorm* approaching.

You will be able to always stay one step ahead of your bitches and doing your best to prevent them from taking the steering wheel of your life.

Knowledge is power.

Imagine if the wrath of Hurricane Bitch was on its way, how could you calmly and rationally respond to the situation? How can you use the "intel" the bitches are giving you to make better decisions in your life or help you discover where you might need to do a little work on yourself?

Origins of *Bitchery*

So, what are YOUR bitches trying to tell you? Whenever you detect those voices showing up, you can pretty much just assume that part of it is coming from straight-up BITCHERY, but that part of it is coming from your true beliefs, feelings, or perceptions. And it usually falls into one of the following five categories.

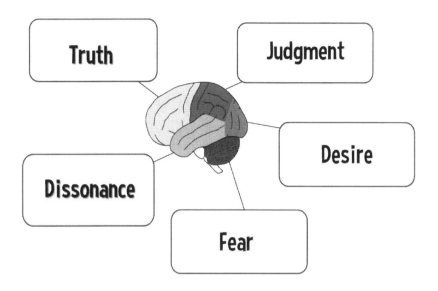

Truth

Even if your self-talk or inner-chatter doesn't come across in the nicest of ways, the bitchery DOES usually stem from bits of truth (even if it's only tiny bits). Like the example of when there's blueberry in your teeth. The bitch would (metaphorically) point and laugh and make a lot of noise about it. But the truth is you *do* still have something in your teeth. The real challenge is simply figuring out which part of what the bitch is saying is *actual* truth, and which part of it is *perceived* truth (Again it's that DATA vs the DRAMA).

Remember: what actually happened and what you SAY about what happened can be two totally different things.

Judgment

The stabs or the cut-downs that come from the bitch are simply judgments and opinions that don't exactly make you feel all warm and fuzzy. But you want to know where those judgments are actually coming from? Yep, you guessed it! YOU! We as humans (especially female humans) are WIRED to judge, compare, or observe our beliefs about something. Judgement can be used as a powerful tool to make decisions. But the distinction lies in where judgement becomes a weapon—when the judgments become unkind and unfair. A weapon of shame, blame, perfectionism (you get the picture). So listen for your judgements of self. And just know that when you hear them, chances are good that the only one judging you is YOU. And until you learn to look at yourself with a little less (unfair) judgment and a little more compassion, you'll be stuck with the nagging feeling that you're being judged all the time.

THINK: How can you use what YOUR Bitches are telling you as information about what you really want to *upgrade* in your own life? How can you have compassion for yourself in the areas that you aren't showing up as your best self and use it to propel yourself forward?

Desire

I want every woman to have everything that she wants. I don't want her to have to make a choice between getting what she wants and her happiness. I want you (and all women) to have more 'AND' in your life.

* ★ Health AND Happiness.
* ★ Get Results AND Enjoy Life
* ★ Accept yourself as you are and for who you are AND go get em' tiger! (Get that body, career, relationship, life that you want!)
* ★ Have less 'OR'...and have more 'AND'.

There is absolutely nothing wrong with desiring anything in your life, but when you place requirements around those desires (requirements to be happy, to move on, to feel like you are *enough*) that's when trouble can arise (aka YOUR Bitches). And unfulfilled desires can easily show itself as jealousy, scarcity, and (GULP!) insecurity. If you can simply become aware and ask yourself if you have unknowingly elevated this desire to a *requirement*, then you'll have the awareness and the power. Desires are inevitable, natural, and fabulous, if you know what they are and what they aren't. Use this part of you to help you figure out what you really *want* and what's just plain owning you, trapping you, or defining you.

Dissonance

We've all been there: "I should be doing this, but I'm doing that," or "I could've done it that way, but I'm doing it this way." When you're living in a world of should'a, would'a, and could'a, there will always be a little Bitch on your shoulder reminding you of what you thought you were 'supposed' to be doing. It's called *cognitive dissonance*, and honestly, this usually leads to guilt, shame, and blame. No bueno. As long as you are making haphazard decisions that aren't in direct alignment with what YOU really want, this part of the Bitch will be showing up regularly. How can you start to get in the habit of noticing when you're doing, saying, or committing to things because you think you 'should' or are 'supposed to', and started asking yourself, "How do I want to feel? And what [action/thought/step] would send me moving in THAT direction"? As long as you are skipping over this important question, then you are always going to act REACTIVELY (instead of intentionally RESPONDING), and your Inner-Bitch is going to come out make you feel like you can't do a single thing right, and she'll always remind you of the "other way". You can also flip this around and use this dissonance that you're experiencing to your advantage. It may also be just the reminder you need to remember you might want to change course – that it FEELS important to you.

Fear

It doesn't take a rocket scientist to figure out that going after what you *really* want can be downright scary! But whether you go after it or not, that fear will still be there. Fear is a natural thing (and it can even be a *good* thing if you look at it for what it is). Fear is the *human* part of you. Not experiencing fear would be like not blinking your eyes. Here's the REAL truth that no one ever told me about fear:

There's never going to be a 'perfect' time for you to make the leap -- to take the plunge. There's never going the 'right moment' for you to rip off the proverbial band-aid and step into your greater future. There's never going to be the 'ideal' set of circumstances you need to make those big shifts in your life. The truth of it all: The fears never fully go away. They'll always be there. Because that's what our brains are WIRED to detect and look for: Fear. Problems. Obstacles. (We have to 'teach it' how to look for the love, the possibilities, the opportunities, gratitude.)

But here's what else you can count on: Your desires, hopes, and dreams will ALSO always be there. Yea it's scary to step into the unknown sometimes -- to overhaul an area of your life in order to take steps towards happiness. But you know what I say about it? It's scarier NOT to! So which one are YOU going to let 'win'? The fear? Or the love?

For me I can honestly say that when I choose the love (Of self, of my life, of my greater future), I'm NEVER sorry. When I choose the fear, I almost ALWAYS am.

So which one are you going to choose? I have a feeling, it' won't be actually be as scary as your brain is making it out to seem. After all what's the alternative? What would happen for you if NOTHING changed? If you stayed on the same path day after day... year after year? Fear and anxiety (and sadness) don't have to win. But YOU have to take the first step. It's up to you.

Where Bitchery Goes Wrong

Knowing and becoming aware of your Inner-Bitches and self-talk isn't enough to make long-term changes. In fact, dabbling in *Ditchery* without really knowing what you are doing can actually make things worse. If you identify and poke a bunch of Bitches with a stick and don't know how to maintain yourself, the repercussions can be horrific.

That's why it's important to not only acquire your own set of Bitch-Detecting skills and capabilities, but to actually be prepared to use them when there is an inevitable Bitch-Storm on deck.

As I mentioned before, if you can get to know your Bitches, learn their language, understand what they are trying to tell you, and then go INFLUENCE yourself so that you 'show up' more powerfully in your life, you'll be golden! ☺

Here are some distinctions to help you understand yourself even more:

Ditch Distinctions

Truth	⟶	**Reality**
Dissonance	⟶	**Danger**
Fear	⟶	**Anxiety**
Judgment	⟶	**Shame**
Desire	⟶	**Require**

Truth vs. Reality:

What **actually** happened and what **you say about** what happened may be two very different things. This is left to the discretion of your perception. Based on some "Geekery" beyond the scope of this topic, we know that our brain's perception is dictated by our past beliefs and past experiences. Often the case is that we are simply a product of the stories we grew up listening to and the "authority" in our lives' view of things. Based on repetition, we just pick up opinions and beliefs of others, and then download them as our own. Especially after a long period of time, it becomes hard to tell whether we actually feel this way or are saying this, or if it's what someone else is feeling or saying (or what we think some-one else is feeling or saying). Because of these reasons, it's really easy to live in this "alternate reality" if we aren't careful.

My own personal go-to question when I want to know who's in charge of my actions?

I simply say: *"Says who?"*

That way I can ask myself: *"Do **I** say this, or is it based on what **someone else** thinks or is saying?"*

I refer to it as my "Reality Check".

A Little Word about the Truth

I wrote the following one afternoon after my encounter with one of my personal bitches. I realized that when there's a bitch in charge, she turns me into a liar! Here's what I wrote:

Wow, I am such a liar!

Sometimes we lie to ourselves about what we really want or what we really don't want, but we are always lying until that day we KNOW how to distinguish one voice from another.

Maybe we aren't straight-up lying, but not telling the whole truth to yourself about yourself is still a lie.

And we get so good at it that we actually believe the things we've been telling ourselves for so long.
I say things to myself like:

You are never going to DO _
You will never BE _
You will never FEEL _

You will always DO _
You will always BE _
You will always FEEL _

How the hell do I know that? How the hell do YOU know that?

I don't. We don't. But I kept believing the lies... until I didn't anymore.

So I asked myself:

If I choose to continue walking around with these magic-crystal-ball certainties, then shouldn't I at least attempt to go prove myself wrong? If we dare make statements like these to ourselves, about ourselves, don't we at least owe it to ourselves to go do the "recon"--especially if it's something that we really, truly, deep down in our heart of hearts want?

So by all means,

- Be realistic
- Take calculated risks
- Be aware of dangers, threats, risks, obstacles, and speed bumps.
- Be practical.
- Use logic and reason.
- Take care of yourself and your well-being.

But go out there and at least attempt to shock yourself! Figure out what lights you up inside and go get em' tiger. It's not mutually exclusive with the above, and they don't cancel each other out.
Dare greatly and don't apologize for what you want.
Live with courage when you require or desire something.
And stay open to the possibility of having your jaw drop down to the floor in amazement, surprise, and delight.

And go prove your "always will" and "never will" statements to be a load of B.S.

Dissonance vs. Danger:

When your brain detects threat, danger, or simply doesn't have full confidence that it is in fact safe, it will (hands-down every time) go into some sort of threat reaction.

If your brain detects imminent threat, it will do one of 3 things:

Fight. Flight. Freeze.

- ★ **Fight**: put your dukes up, raise your voice, get defensive or argumentative
- ★ **Flight**: Run Away. Quit. Go quickly and easily from black to white—either "all in" or "all out". Start things and don't finish them. Not say anything—not share what's on your mind. Hide. Seek safety. Numb your pain with anything from TV to chocolate.
- ★ **Freeze**: I'm afraid to take a step this way or this way. I don't know which way to go, so I'm not going to go anywhere.

But here's the thing: If you have *Bitches* in your life that are in the driver's seat, you are essentially going around reacting and not responding to your life, things are always going to seem a bit "off".

If you aren't wearing your *Reality Goggles*, your brain doesn't know that you're simply feeling confused or something's unclear. It would actually think you are in DANGER and will trigger that Threat Response.

Boom! **Fight, Flight, Freeze.**

Take your pick.

Imagine if instead you simply practiced responding to the situation when something confuses you. Imagine if every time you caught yourself making a knee-jerk reaction by running away or getting feisty, you simply said:

> *"Whoa there, wait a minute. What exactly doesn't feel right? Where do I not have the information I need to respond?"*

Then you can decide if sticking around to get that information is worth it. See how you would be having a completely different conversation and a completely different outcome?

Fear vs. Anxiety:

Bitches come around when fear shows up only if skip over a very important step: identifying and acknowledging the fear itself.

Here's the thing that I think most women don't realize: Even if you were the most confident, self-assured person in the world, it does not mean that getting faced with obstacles, variables, and fear magically stop.

What's different about the aforementioned kind of woman however is how she handles the fear as it shows up?

The 2 most common occurrences I see:

1. Ignore the fear, hope it will go away.
2. See the fear, pretend it doesn't mean anything or doesn't matter, and then essentially ignore it.

But neither of these scenarios will serve you. In fact they'll just prolong the threat.

I believe it's imperative it is to actually assume that "threat" will in fact be there, but commit to preparing yourself to be able to handle it.

If you looked at it just like that-- that fear was going to come up in your life time and time again and that there was no possible way to avoid it, but that you also had the ability to choose whether you **reacted** or **responded** to it—wouldn't that change the game?

Judgment vs. Shame:

Everyone makes judgments every day. We as humans are WIRED to do so. We are constantly judging how we feel about other things, people, and beliefs. When we judge ourselves and others without compassion however, that's when it can turn into a recipe for shame. If we don't love who we are being or who we might have been in our past, it sends us down a road of shame.

If you hear the jabs and put-downs from the Bitches that seem harsh or out of line, it might simply be YOU judging YOU without compassion and understanding. This is when it can get ugly. Chances are good that the only one judging you is YOU, so until you learn to look at yourself with a little less judgment and a little more compassion, you'll be stuck with the nagging feeling that you're being judged all the time.

Instead of asking yourself whether you are judging yourself or shaming yourself, you can even keep it as simple as asking yourself if you feel that you are being FAIR to yourself. It's an easy way to tell the difference between the judgments you might face. Then you can figure out how to have compassion for yourself in the areas that you aren't showing up as your best self and use it to propel yourself forward.

Desire Vs. Require

Let's say a man brings flowers home for his wife every single Friday. At first she is delighted. She knows he doesn't have to bring them for her, but she really appreciates it, and she grows to actually start expecting them.

One day the man is running late and stuck in traffic and doesn't have time to stop and pick up flowers for his wife.

When he walks in empty handed, immediately she starts thinking:

"What's wrong? Did I do something? Is he not attracted to me anymore? Is there someone else?"

She loved getting flowers and she **desired** to get them every single Friday, but she never made it a **requirement** for her husband. She simply loved getting the flowers and desired that it continued.

Unbeknownst to her though, she started relying on the expectation that flowers would be part of every Friday afternoon, and it gradually moved from a *desire* to a *requirement* in her mind. Now whenever he didn't bring her flowers, she assumed the worst. In her mind her husband was no longer meeting the requirements that showed her that he loved her, was faithful to her, or any other number of things she imagined in her mind that the flowers represented.

In reality though, none of her assumptions or stories were true. The lack of flowers that one afternoon was simply a product of circumstance. But because she unknowingly elevated the flowers from *desire* to *require*, her perception completely changed.

So where in your life are you saying that something is a requirement and actually treating it like it's a desire? Where are you doing the opposite?

There is absolutely nothing wrong with desiring anything in your life, but when you place requirements around those desires (requirements to be happy, to move on, to feel like you are *enough*) that is when your personal Bitches will show up at your doorstep.

The 4 Sides To Every Story

We've all heard that there are 3 sides to every story, but I believe there are actually 4 sides to every story.

- ★ The Bitch Story
- ★ The Ditch Story
- ★ Your Story
- ★ The ReStory

The *Bitch Story* is the version that paints you as seen through the eyes of your biggest critic, your biggest naysayer, or your trusty enabler.

The *Ditch Story* is the version that paints you as seen through the eyes of your best friend. It's the wisdom or advice your Fairy Stepsister (from another Mister) would give you. Total belief and support and love. Unconditionally acceptance, connection, and care. The utmost know, like, and trust.

Your Story is the version that paints you as seen through your current goggles. It's the story of what actually happened (The Data). And then there's the meaning, justification, explanation or story that YOU give it (The Drama). This can vary based on how you feel about yourself at any given particular moment.

When I'm having a 'fat' day or a not-so-confident day, my stories follow suit. On any given day, your story is a product of a mixture of your biggest Bitch and your most loving B.F.F. And then there is the *ReStory*.

The ReStory is the version of your story that you can retell at any time. It's your version of events in hindsight, with experiential wisdom, and without any goggles on at all.

Perhaps it's the version of the story that you would have lived in real-time had you known what you know now. It's the Truth (with a Capital T).

And the best thing about the *ReStory* is that it's never too late to go back and tell **your** *ReStory*, and it's never too early to start living inside of **your** *ReStory*.

The 3 Breeds of Bitch (And Their Stories)

Self-Image Bitches: The Bitches that impact what you say and what you see **to** yourself and **about** yourself. They penetrate your long-held beliefs of yourself – the ultimate story of who you think you are.

Self-Esteem Bitches: The Bitches that impact how well you know, like, and trust yourself. And this in turn impacts how much you trust yourself to actually follow through on the promises you make to yourself. They penetrate your habits, behaviors, and choices (and how you feel about yourself as a reflection).

Body-Image Bitches: The Bitches that impact what you see and what you say about your body, your fat, and food (and how you feel about yourself in relation to it). They run the 'racket' of your default story about your body (how it does or doesn't look, feel, move, appear, or perform)

Self-Image Bitches

These are the bitches of the house, the head honchos, and the ring leaders of them all. These bitches have been in charge a very long time—possibly your whole life.

The self-image bitches are in charge of what you think about yourself, and what you say about yourself (to yourself). And let's just say that they don't typically go about it in the kindest or gentlest ways.

They are always telling you what others are probably thinking or might be thinking of you, instead of asking you what *you* think about you.

And they say the stuff to you that you wouldn't say to your worst enemy. They are fine saying things to you that would ruin any real-life relationship.

- ★ Judging you with *zero* compassion.
- ★ Telling you that you aren't worthy of love and happiness and a life you love.
- ★ Talking your ear off with typical Bitchery, belittling, and 'smack-talk'.

But that's not even the worst part of it. The worst thing is their tone, their demeanor, and the authority and power they command. They speak so matter-of-factly and so condescendingly (like they are the expert or something!) that we often don't even think about the fact that they might be wrong. We don't even take it into consideration that maybe they've been misled, misinformed, or are just simply incorrect.

Your Self-Image

Years ago I stumbled across a book called Psycho-Cybernetics written by a plastic surgeon named Maxwell Maltz. Women and men would come into his office swearing that their big nose, minimally endowed chest, or vicious scar made them ugly— that it was ruining their lives and killing their hopes and dreams.

They swore that plastic surgery would solve their problems, make their lives worth living, or help them achieve all they ever dreamed of. So Maxwell Maltz performed nose jobs, breast augmentations, and scar removals left and right. Some were pleased with the results, but most came back still internally distraught.

Maltz would hold up a mirror during the post-op checkup and show the new-nosed woman his handywork (the new nose she had begged him for, the nose she showed a picture of to emulate, the nose that was supposedly the answer to her problems)....

But instead of feeling ecstatic with his work, she was distraught, deflated, and still self-loathing.

When she looked in the mirror, even though she was staring at a completely different reflection, she STILL saw the same thing. She STILL thought she had a big nose. She STILL felt ugly and saw that "ugly" in the mirror.

Same thing happened to the guy with the scar and the woman who now had a more well-endowed set of breasts.

Maltz soon realized that their body "shortcomings" weren't the real problem....

It was their mind. It was their **perception** of their body that was really doing the damage to their Self-Image.

He realized that if he really wanted to help people on the whole— to really fulfill his role as a doctor to the core — he had to figure out the other side of it.

He wanted to figure out what was going on (or not going on) inside their minds that created such distorted perceptions and such skewed versions of reality.

So he researched and poured his heart n' soul into it and came up with what is now referred to as "Psycho Cybernetics"— the Science of the Self-Image.

Soon people were coming to him with typical plastic surgery requests, but instead of operating right away, he would offer them great prices and deals if they complied to his requests:

"Go practice these mental training exercises for the next 30 days, and if you still want the surgery, I'll give you the special deal".

Shortly thereafter he moved away from the world of plastic surgery and focused his efforts on sharing "Psycho Cybernetics" with the rest of the world up until the day he died.

I've probably read this book about 10 different times now, and every time I do, I extract a new nugget of wisdom. Or I simply see something that I didn't see before.

Bottom line though: his work is what made me realize that (for me) it would never matter how "skinny", "successful", or "accomplished" I was. If I didn't change how I was seeing myself on the inside, nothing I created on the outside would even matter.

That's because I was (and always will be) searching for a feeling. And nothing outside of ourselves can make us feel how we want to feel on the inside. Maybe it will for a little while, but after that wears off, you'll always end up right back at your default. That default IS your Self-Image.

So now I turn it over to you:

Where are you still looking for something outside of you — going after weight loss, dieting, making more money, attaining some quantifiable or "shiny object" — without ever addressing the cause that's coming from the inside?

Because I will tell you this with the utmost certainty:

As long as you continue addressing everything outside yourself or outside of your body, you"ll continue to use the THINKING of the "same brain that created the problem".

That means you'll continue to walk around with the same Self-Image, the same Self-Esteem, and the same Body-Image.

More importantly you'll have the same internal conversations and the same BodyTalk.

And until that shifts, change will continue to be short-lived, temporary, and ever-fleeting. More of the same will go IN, and more of the same outcomes will come OUT.

Sure the tactics, the quantifiables, and the modalities might change. But the THINKING will be exactly the same.

You love yourself (and anything) to the degree that you are caring, connecting, and accepting. And if changing your body, losing some weight, or making more money will make you feel any of those things, then by all means, go for it — I support anything that will truly make you a better version of yourself!

But don't forget to change the INSIDE as well as the OUTSIDE while you go.

Go in the direction of love on your way there — not in the direction of self-loathing, non-stop guilt, shame, blame, and comparing yourself to anything or anyone BUT yourself.

Love yourself happy. Love yourself healthy!

Because then….you get to actually be HAPPY!

If I could go back and tell my younger self, my 'fat' self, or my 'ignorant' self any advice, it would be this:

Don't just change how you look on the OUTSIDE. Change how you feel on the INSIDE.

Those aren't just some fancy shmancy words I'm using to make a point or sound insightful. It's what I know to be true. And it's all I want for you too.

So What's the Solution?

If I were to nutshell what I just said it would be that (I believe) you need to go from:

* ★ Feeling powerless to taking responsibility of your own happiness, purpose, and meaning.

* ★ Feeling powerless to feeling fully connected to THAT responsibility, and feeling like you have ownership of your life.

* ★ Feeling DISempowered to feeling like you know how to find your own source of empowerment.

But in order to actually achieve this, there are a few necessary steps (ingredients) that I know to be necessary for you to go through:

The 5 Ingredients to Self-Love (and An UNshakeable Self-Image)

* ★ **Self-Care:** Figuring out what it would take for you to care for yourself (as a verb and a noun) physically, mentally, socially/emotionally.

★ **Self-Acceptance:** Figuring out what it would look like/feel like for you to fully accept yourself without exception? (This really crosses over with the whole connection and care piece of the puzzle.)

★ **Self-Worth:** Reconciling your past experiences and helping you find the value in what you're currently devaluing or experiencing shame around. Helping you figure out what you are 'weighing', what you are measuring to account for your self-worth... and what it would take to go fill that gap.

★ **Self-Esteem:** Understanding the know, like, and trust factor of yourself. Because chances are that currently you are relinquishing that to someone else. Other people are telling you who you are. Other people are telling you why you should or shouldn't like yourself, and other people and circumstances are dictating whether or not you trust yourself. 'Upping' that know like trust factor. Earning back your own trust through the promises that you make and the promises that you keep, and who you want to be in relation to that.

★ **Self-Endorsement:** Figuring out who you are regardless of what anyone else thinks. Because it's not practical or feasible for any of us to "not give a shit" what other people think about us, but IS possible is to figure out what would it take for YOU to value your own opinion of yourself moreso (even just a little bit moreso) than someone else. What would it be like if you didn't need endorsement from someone else to tell you who you are or tell you how much you're worth or tell you how beautiful or desireable you are (or if you have 'the right' to feel that for yourself). What would your champion'ed self look like? What would your proud self look like, talk like, walk like, think like, feel like? Defining that.

THAT all adds up to love. THAT creates your Self-Image that you walk around with, inside, and behind every second ever every single day...for the rest of your life.

Self-Esteem Bitches

The Self-Esteem Bitches will do whatever they have to do to keep you feeling lost and confused and 'out of control'. They cause you to *react* instead of *respond*, and cause you to believe that you are not the one in 'control' of your life – that your life (and its momentum) are officially running YOU. The Self-Esteem Bitches tend to swoop in and steal your independence, your feelings of influence, and your confidence in your abilities.

They will always try to convince you to make decisions that seem to get you out of pain the fastest, put the best band-aid on the situation, or that will 'tide you over' in the short-run. They have no care or concern for how this will affect you long-term.

They have you running around making haphazard commitments and decisions without even consulting with you to figure out if it's in alignment with the direction you want to head.

They get you so frustrated and fed up with the effects of your actions and lack of results that you throw in the towel. This happens so often that you mistakenly confuse it with a motivation or willpower problem, or lack of accountability.

And in turn, every time this happens (every time you make a promise to yourself and witness yourself "dropping the ball"), it causes you to trust and believe in yourself less and less.

They feed off of your lack of inspiration or clarity. And they keep doing it until you feel so out of control of your life, so confused about where you should go or what you should do that you are constantly looking for someone else to fill in the blanks for you.

Pretty soon you have lost all ability to trust in yourself to make the best decisions without third-party backup, and you no longer have your "gut" to rely on.

Now your life officially owns *you.*

The Self-Esteem Bitches feed on that doubt and that lack of trust in yourself. This is where they are most powerful. Not only do you feel weak when these bitches are around, but you now also have a series of habits that have laid themselves down to keep you *reacting* to situations with a lack of clarity.

What should you wear that day? Oh, you aren't able to make that decision on your own. You need to consult a third party.

Which one should you choose? Oh you aren't capable of making decisions on your own. You need to consult someone with more expertise.

Which plan is the best plan for you? Pshhhh, nothing has worked in the past. What makes you think you are qualified to make these decisions now? You need to consult your best friend, your hair-stylist, or your dog walker's cousin's friend.

Where do you want to go? Who do you want to be? How do you want to feel? You aren't able to decide that for yourself! Not without finding out from someone else what you are "supposed" to do.

Go ask anyone else. Chances are they know more than you.

These Bitches will leave you so hooked and strung out on third party motivation, accountability, and willpower that you will think that you can't do anything on your own.

So What's the Solution?

Remember: everything is a story. If there's a current story in your brain that is sending your self-esteem on a downward spiral, you must go back and change it.

But in order to do that, you have to let go of who you THINK you are (or ways of being that you've had for a very long time), and give yourself permission to go back and earn back your own trust!

Because if you get brutally honest with yourself, I think you'll find that your relationship with yourself has become NEGOTIABLE.

Don't feel bad about this. It's SO much more common than you think. And it's a natural occurrence when you think about it.

Why does this happen? What causes us to become entangled in a negotiable relationship with ourselves?
- ★ Making promises that you don't want to make
- ★ Making promises you don't want to keep
- ★ Making promises that you can't keep

We ALL do it. We all fall into this trap.

We want to do it all, have it all, be it all, right?

And simply creating an *Awareness Awareness* around the promises that you make and the promises that you keep is the first step to starting over and earning back your own trust.

Just think about it: Non-Negotiable Promises:

What would that look like, feel like, sound like? Who would you be if your word became NON-negotiable?

Body-Image Bitches

This is the type of Bitch that causes you to think you feel ugly or fat, or tells you you're not sexy, beautiful, glowing, gorgeous, elegant, desirable, fill-in-the-blank.

They are the ones that make you actually believe that:

- ★ You *are* your unbutton able jeans.
- ★ Your body is wrong or bad or broken.
- ★ You have fat—therefore you *are* fat.
- ★ Your body is not the one you want. And who would want *your* body?
- ★ Your body is you and you are your body
- ★ Your body is your heart, your soul
- ★ Your body is your *worth*

They are the ones that look back at you from your reflection in the mirror and blatantly abuse you:

- ★ Eek that does *not* look good!
- ★ You look so *fat* in that outfit.
- ★ Your hair is a big ol' mess and is frizzing like you just put your hand in an electric socket.
- ★ When people see that, they will think you're totally gross. Nobody will want you.
- ★ You are so ugly!

They are the ones that look in the mirror and pick apart every single feature, every single asset, and look for the things that aren't perfect, that aren't pretty, and that aren't "good enough".

★ Your boobs are too small
★ No wait! Your boobs are way too big
★ Your hips are hanging over your jeans
★ No wait! You have no hips whatsoever—you look like a little girl
★ Your ass is HUGE—does that thing have its own zip code?
★ You have no ass. It's like the back of your body is flat.
★ Yuck! I see cellulite!
★ Your eyes are dull and small and an ugly color.
★ Your stomach makes you look pregnant.
★ Your toes are weird.
★ Your nose looks like a big hook.
★ You've always been fat, and you'll always be fat.

They are the ones whispering MADNESS in your ear about what your "fat ass" needs to go do to "fix" things!

★ Don't eat that! You'll gain weight!
★ No pain, no gain. Just work through it.
★ You need to do more! More! More! More!
★ Just don't eat anything. I saw this cleanse on Dr. Oz where one lady lost 15 pounds in 20 minutes!

The real kicker is that they are the ones actually KEEPING your body from changing! Telling you things like:

- ★ You've tried this a million times; this time won't be any different.
- ★ Maybe you just aren't cut out to ever have that kind of body.
- ★ Just quit. This shit is HARD! And it's not worth it!
- ★ Just eat it. You can start back up again on Monday.
- ★ It won't matter anyway. It doesn't ever make a difference.
- ★ The reason you're unhappy with your life is because of your body.

The Body Bitches will do anything they can, working hand-in-hand with the Self-Image and Self-Esteem Bitches, to keep you feeling shame and agony over the body of yours—and they won't let you anywhere near the biggest secret of all: that the amazing body you have is ALREADY *perfectly imperfect*.

So What's the Solution?

Here's the truth:

There's no ONE solution. There's simply YOUR solution. So all I can do is share what the process and journey looked like for me, and then invite you to find YOUR new story.

Talk to me or hang out with me, and it's very clear to see that:

★ I am VERY comfortable in my body.
★ I am VERY comfortable around food (even around the things women think they're not 'supposed' to eat)

★ I'm VERY comfortable being me (and trust me, I have a lot of 'weird' quirks and eccentricities that used to make me anything but proud of who I am).

This is who I am now, but it's not who I always was.

But you can learn any new 'way of being' if you decide it to be so — if you choose it.

Because EVERYTHING is a skill.

We become good at whatever we practice — whatever we give attention and repetition to.

And we can DEFINITELY place intentional focus and direction towards whatever it is that we want to become 'good' at.

For me it was no different.

★ I HATED how I felt about myself in my body.
★ I HATED how I felt about myself around food (before, during, and after I ate)
★ I HATED how I felt about myself on the inside — how I treated myself with my words and my actions.

So I went out and intentionally changed those ways of being that I didn't approve of (and want to accept from myself) any longer.

I intentionally practiced those changes until they became me — until I transformed.

And I believe that YOU are no different. I was about as fargone and disconnected from my body as you could be. Crazy-addictive/controlling tendencies with food. Uber-critical and punishing relationship with my body. Outright abusive and loathing relationship with self.

So yea, I may seem like I see the world in rainbow-colored unicorns, but I truly believe that if I can do it, so can you.

So what's my answer for those that ask me "How did YOU do it?"

Well here's what I would say about it today:

★I Learned How To EAT★

I went back and got 'right' with food. I got 'right' with my emotional (over)eating, and I learned how to feed my body what it needs so it is happy (all year long) and makes my job keeping it lean-(ish), fit-(ish), and pain-free super-simple and super-doable and fun!

★I Learned How To PLAY★

I went back and got 'right' with my body. I got 'right' with my fat. I called a truce. I decided to stop berating it, ignoring it, abusing it, and overworking it, and I learned how to CARE for it.

We became friends, partners-in-crime to do all the things I never tried or was sitting on the sidelines wishing I had, and I went and PLAYED.

I learned how to paddle board, ice skate, roller skate, became friends with nature, started dancing, acted like a kid again, became a 'girly girl', and set myself (and my body free) after 30 years of feeling trapped. And if I can do it, so can you.

★I Learned How To LOVE ★

I went back and made amends with this idea that I've been being a bitch to myself my whole life, and that even though we are indeed wired to judge other people and ourselves (and that I've practiced it my whole life), that it doesn't just change or go away overnight.

It's a process. It's a life-long commitment where I have to pass through a few stages. I need to get to know myself, trust myself, and pass through 'like' to get to love. It's a process. One foot in front of the other. Same days are harder than others. But getting back up is NON-negotiable. Me, myself, and I are together for the rest of our lives whether I like it or not. We are together forever. That's one thing I CAN count on and predict. So I can choose to work WITH myself or AGAINST myself. But I realized that I DO have a choice.

★I Learned How To LIVE ★

I went back and drew that line in the sand and decided I wasn't going to miss out on my life any more. I wasn't going to hate my experience of life just to get the body, the beauty, or the bank account that I (thought I) wanted. That burning myself out, exhausting myself, and sucking the life out of me was NOT worth it to obtain any jean size or $ sign, and that my own CARE and my own HAPPINESS needs to come first. Or the other people that I want to give it to will continue to have to "wait in line".

Bottom Line: I decided that my old way of living was NOT how and who I wanted to be anymore. And I chose something new. I wasn't sure what it looked like at the time, but I didn't care. I knew I needed to step into SOMETHING new or else I would keep 'feeding' the version of myself I knew would destroy me and keep me in a cycle of pain, doubt, lack, and stuckness.

Because again:

♥ You can CHOOSE (today!) to declare that you are finished with the beating yourself up, rejecting yourself, and giving yourself shit because you're not at a certain weight.

♥ You can CHOOSE (today!) to end the 'war' you're in against yourself (and each of us have our own unique war that we waged once upon a time) and lay down the 'weapons' of shame and blame and comparison and perfectionism that are keeping you from living in the 'now' of your life — they keep you stuck in the past or fearful of the future, and they further lead to you REJECTING you.

❤ You can CHOOSE (today!) to make this DAY 1 of a kinder, loving, more compassionate approach to 'dealing' with yourself, to transforming your body, to anything really.

Because what's the alternative? And how long have you been trying out THAT alternative? And how is THAT working for you? I'd bet my money that it's NOT working for you.

You do have a choice. YOU are the ONE thing you can 'control'. But you have to CHOOSE it. You have to choose stepping into a newer version of yourself and a new way of being.

You DO have a choice. What will you choose?

Part 3:
HOW TO DITCH THE BITCH

How to Ditch the Bitch (Made Simple)

We ALL have bitches (or so I believe).

They may have different names, different faces, and come out in different circumstances, but here's what's always true:

We all have our own special blend and own special 'recipe'.

We can either fight them, believe them, resist them, or ignore them. Or we can accept that they are indeed there and that:

- ★ They bring a story with them (THEY bring the drama)
- ★ They are your unfair and unkind judgements about yourself (and the judgements will never go away, but you can start being mindful of the kind of judgements you're making)
- ★ They are *Ditch*-able! As in, you can become the version of yourself that isn't so impacted by them, and YOU can become the version of yourself that has **the most** influence over your life and how you feel.

And in order to do that, here's what needs to happen NOW and moving forward:

1. Accept that YOU have Bitches and get to know them. (This book is the first step in doing just that.) Create (what I call) an *Awareness Awareness* -- and really start learning to understand them and (in turn) understand YOU! Don't fight them. Don't resist them. And don't try to mentally 'kill' them. Start being of aware of them and what they are saying. Then start to decipher what they are ACTUALLY saying.
2. Know them and seek to understand them.

3. Take these new *Awareness Awarenesses* and let them permeate into the inner-workings of your brain. And then go and influence YOU. Influence who you're being, what you're doing, and how you're feeling by getting yourself involved in a *Winning Game* Plan with *Winning* Experiments -- one that's designed for the individual that you are, not for the 'widget' that you're not.

4. Go about the 'business' of your life with all of your new *Awareness Awarenesses* -- especially how you're talking **to** yourself, **about** yourself.

We've talked in detail about the first 2 steps (and you'll be get access to more tools to help you continue those processes). Now let's talk about influencing YOU.

For purposes of this book, you are going to hear me refer to 3 main distinctions. Get to know them. Understand them. Study them.

It's in these three distinctions that your power actually lives: either live with the bitches running your life or *ditch* them.

★ The *Experiment Mentality* vs. The *Factory Mentality*
★ *Experiences* vs. *Results*
★ *Winning Game* vs. A *Losing Game*

Knowing these distinctions will enable you to:
★ See where your Bitches are showing up
★ Know WHY they are showing up
★ Know how to get them to leave—or how to disarm them
★ Set yourself up for less Bitchery in the future.

The reason these are so important is because they actually dictate whether or not your plan of attack is a hidden *Bitch-Magnet.*

Referring back to our two stories from before:

> ★ **The *Bitchery* Version**: How things go down in life when the Bitches are around.
> ★ **The *Ditchery* Version:** The way things could go down if you send your Bitch-Detecting self back in time to help your younger self see what she didn't see.

So now that you do have this insight and new awareness around what's going on as you go about the 'business' of your life, I want to create a whole new awareness:

There's nothing 'wrong' with YOU! But...how you might be going about things could potentially be keeping you in that cycle of 'insanity'. Let's take a look.

Are You Stepping In Your Own Pooh?

Throughout my coaching career and on a regular basis in conversations in my everyday life, it's fairly often that someone says:

"Wait, how old are you?"

I've always kind of been an *old soul,* and a lot of my friends have decades on me.

Now anybody that knows me or simply hangs out with me for five minutes surely knows that I say just as many 13-year-old teenage boy remarks as I do insightful and intelligent things.

I'm no Doogie Howser M.D. or genius freak of nature, but I am often accused of being "wise for my years".

When someone tells me that, of course it makes me feel warm and fuzzy inside, but it's not for the reasons that you might think it would.

When someone tells me I'm 'wise', it makes me feel like maybe I have given them a perspective they've never seen or taught them about something that they didn't already know.

To me, wisdom comes from a combination of knowledge and experience – not IQ or intellect. I can easily go learn the in's and out's of something, give you text book definitions and academic theories until I'm blue in the face, and technically "master" a subject when it's in 2-dimensional form in my life, yet have NO practical understanding of the subject at hand.

Take marriage for example. I could study psychology, behavioral sciences, and the actual in's and out's of marriage in textbook form and go become somewhat of an expert on the subject of marriage. But as far as marriage mastery comes (is that an oxymoron?), I have no practical knowledge to draw from, so my expertise is limited.

So how did I become so "wise"?

Jokingly I would tell you it's because I have had so many areas in my life that were 'messed up', or so many areas of my life that I feel or felt a bit 'crazy', and that I have a lot of experience in how to go *clean up* those areas.

My non-joking self would probably give you a similar answer– yet kinder and gentler and with less judgment and more love. Something like:

"I faced many challenges and obstacles personally, professionally, emotionally... and I chose to go face them head-on and commit to mastery".

Then my street-slang rapper-wannabee self might say:

"I simply went back and cleaned up all my shit!"

So whichever version of me you want to accept an answer from, the truth is simple. I went back and assessed all the areas of my life that I wasn't fully happy with. I went through them one by one, figured out where my 'sticking' points were, created an awareness and a mental note to look for THOSE showing up in my life, and then I made adjustments either in the habits or in how I talked to myself about myself...and simply cleaned up the 'mess' that was there.

Think about it: If you take your dog for a walk and DON'T clean up the mess he makes on the side of street, SOMEONE is going to walk in it, right? It might be you, it might not be you, but someone WILL step in it. To me, looking at my own 'mess' on the side of the street and simply walking by it was a guarantee that I would step in it again. And when the mess got too 'painful' for me to step in one more day, that's when I knew I was ready to go clean it up.

And wow, I've cleaned up A LOT of 'messes'.

- ★ My body
- ★ My confidence
- ★ My self-esteem
- ★ My self-worth
- ★ My relationship with food
- ★ My relationship with men
- ★ My relationship with love... period... giving and receiving
- ★ My relationship with owning my life
- ★ My relationship with shame

And yes, I really could go on, and on, and on...

So where are you looking at areas of your life and simply choosing to step in dog pooh every single day?

Where are you noticing that there is something giving you resistance, adding stress or threat, or simply making you feel less than you want to feel? And where are you choosing to ignore it?

I didn't get "wise" from passing by the dog poo every day and doing nothing about it (or worse) complaining about it like I didn't know it was there.

No way!

I have and I will continue to face my challenges head-on and upgrade my life little by little, big by big. But only I can decide when I'm ready for the next upgrade when I've reached my limit of cleaning (metaphorical) dog pooh off my shoes.

And THAT is where true wisdom comes from: the experience-- the actual process of (not just knowing but) KNOWING what it feels like. It's letting all of your senses know what it feels like. You can't experience something just from knowledge alone.

So (and pun DEFINITELY intended), I double dog dare you to ask yourself where you are stepping in the same pile of _____ every single day? And what would it take for you to simply *stop* stepping in it and go clean it up?

This is essentially how I want you to look at all of your beliefs and habits.

The Widget Factory

Let's say someone gave you a new gadget or gizmo that made your life easier, more efficient, and saved you time and energy, but they didn't give you an instruction manual to tell you how to work the thing.

Sure, you've had similar gadgets in your past, but you've never seen one quite like this before. It's not like any others you've seen before, and an instruction manual from another machine WOULDN'T help you understand the complexities of this one.

So imagine if you tried to change anything in your own life—YOUR life that has its own 'bells and whistles' and complexities-- but you did it with the WRONG instruction manual?

THAT is exactly how most people approach change or life upgrades. They use an instruction manual that was designed for someone else completely, and then wonder why they didn't get the results they were looking for.

I call this the *Factory Mentality*. I originally came up with this term when I was working in the fitness industry.

Over the years I've read 100's of books. You name it: any fitness book I could find, nutrition and food methods, think positive, psychology, brain science and pain science.

Eat **less** in a world where you're already hungry. Move **more** doing something you hate. Add in **more** to your already overstuffed and exhausted schedule. Just do whatever the experts are saying.

And they would essentially say that if you didn't train even harder, eat even less, and think even more positively, then it's YOUR fault it didn't work-- that you must be a self-sabotager, weak- willed or didn't want it badly enough.

But hold up! This was actually what the people I was working with (mainly women trying to lose weight and "tone up") had been doing all along! They already did the "eat less move more", try harder song and dance for most of their lives, and it didn't get them anywhere.

It wasn't giving them endless amounts of energy and making them feel physically unstoppable like the books promised. And that mirror they would inevitably look straight in the eye each day? It wasn't telling them that they were lovely and beautiful and should be proud of what they saw staring back.

And their relationships with themselves and other people— they weren't making them ooze with excitement and confidence like the back cover said they would.

Unfortunately though THAT is when most people decide that their investment of time, money heart and soul REALLY wasn't worth it, and it's time to throw in the towel. Or maybe they stopped looking for a better way period and simply accepted their 'fate' to keep traveling down same road, day in, day out.

Of course they didn't love their life. They were constantly paying the price, but never actually getting to see the goods! They never had anything to show for it. After all, they DID pay for them right? They did what the book told them to do until they simply couldn't do it anymore. And I believe it's because they had been getting their "goods" from the *Factory* for way too long.

You know the *Factory*. The **same** assembly line where the **same** thing goes in, and the **same** thing comes out, over and over again. Same mold, same process. You can't tell a difference from one plastic widget to the next.

But wait a minute, we aren't widgets! Why would anyone make decisions in their life treating themselves like a widget?

Are you the same as everyone else you know?

Same weight? Same height? Same build? Same beliefs? Same fears, dreams, hopes, desires?

Then why would you go to the same *Factory* as your neighbor, your hairdresser, your cousin's dog-walker, or your best friend?

Wouldn't it make more sense to ditch the production-line mentality and try something that was actually designed with **you** in mind (or even BETTER) designed by **your** mind?

That is the difference between the *Factory Mentality* and the *Experiment Mentality*.

As long as you are living your life as a widget, Bitches will show up and haunt you. They actually feed off the Factory Mentality, and they almost always win.

With the Factory Mentality there's always:

★ Other people's opinions weighing in and making decisions

★ Repeat of past failures without stopping to change course

★ Endless needs for drip-feeds of motivation. If you're always doing whatever you think you "should" be doing, you'll always need that push to keep going.

And I believe that as soon as you stop approaching your goals like you were a factory-created exact replica of every other woman in the world, you're going to find that suddenly you don't feel so lost or stuck, suddenly you don't even need to rely on willpower or accountability, and suddenly you'll start actually enjoying the experience of your life while you get there.

You'll notice that everything within the contents of this book has been designed to help YOU create your own Mad Science Experiment—to help you create YOUR ideal life.

Hypothetically Speaking

The *Factory Mentality* isn't just about the Bitches either. It comes down to asking yourself if you are going down the path that's right for you. Does it take you closer towards your desires and goals? Does it help you enjoy your experience of life more? And how do you FEEL on your way?

Imagine you just won a contest or a raffle and you were awarded a dream vacation package as the grand prize. All expenses paid. 5 star accommodations. All the food and drink you could possibly want. Perfect weather for all the excursions. A dream come true, right?

Now imagine finding out that this "dream vacation" was bound for a winter ski trip in the mountains in Colorado. Your 5 star accommodations were booked at a beautiful log cabin with the best views around. There was a constant flow of meats, cheeses, the finest chocolates, and the best wine money could buy. The ground was covered in snow—perfect for getting out on the slopes and taking advantage. Sounds perfect right?

Well for someone it might be...

But imagine if you hated the cold weather with a fiery passion. Imagine if you were allergic to all types of natural wood and sneezed and itched from the second you stepped foot in the cabin. Imagine if you were a vegan and wouldn't eat any of the delicacies provided. And imagine if you had a sprained ankle and couldn't step foot on the slopes even if you wanted to.

Still sound like YOUR dream vacation?

This is what we do when it comes to seeking out our "perfect" plan for anything we want to transform or upgrade. We take a plan that was created with one person in mind, and mesh it into our own lives and circumstances—even if it's practically the WORST plan possible for us. Then (duh!) it ends up becoming a complete failure.

So what do we do next? We find the next "perfect" plan that was designed for someone else. And the next one, and the next one...

See a pattern being repeated here?

If you had the chance to get your hands on a dream vacation, wouldn't you want it to be your dream vacation? I mean if you were handed something that had absolutely no use to you, do you think it would make a difference? In a way, it would be like it never existed to begin with.

'Mad Science'

Factory thinking is designed to get you results. Results are awesome. I love getting results. But you know what I don't love? I don't love the *Bounceback Effect* that inevitably takes place when I try to get crazy results that are impossible to maintain because of the crazy way I got them.

You see most programs are designed to work when you actually follow the program, but what happens when you stop following the program'?

And let's face it: eventually you will stop following the program at some point right? No one gets everything right on the first try or 100% of the time.

Merely getting results is not the solution to becoming your best self. Results are important, but you've got to make sure that they don't deceive you either.

Do you remember the Scientific Method? (And no, this isn't some pop quiz to see if you remember high school physics), but you may be underestimating the power of the good ol' Scientific Method to help you make massive changes in your life.

Here's the part about it though that most people don't realize: **You are already using it!**

> **ACCORDING TO WIKIPEDIA:** The *Scientific Method* is a body of techniques for investigating phenomena, acquiring new knowledge, or correcting and integrating previous knowledge. The chief characteristic which distinguishes the *Scientific Method* from other methods of acquiring knowledge is that the scientists seek to let **REALITY** speak for itself, supporting a theory when a theory's predictions are confirmed, and challenging a theory when its predictions prove false.

Yep, you might not be aware of it, but you are using it every time you start anything – whether you know it or not!

The bad news is that most people are using the method based on **old** and **outdated** information– beliefs that you have about yourself or are based on past "failures"—and beliefs that don't serve you and the person you want to become!

Plus, on top of that, I actually believe you've been asking the **wrong** questions all along. I mean if you're going to be using it anyways, you might as well learn how to use it to your advantage right?

Here's how to use an *Experiment Mentality* to start getting where you want to go VERY quickly. Think about it like this:

* **PRE-EXPERIMENT FIELD RESEARCH:** Use your past experiences and attempts as DATA and RESEARCH to go craft the best *Experiment* for YOU and YOUR life

* **QUESTION**: The question will always be: Does this work for ME?

* **HYPOTHESIS**: Ideally the hypothesis will always be YESSS! Remember, you wouldn't create the upcoming *Experiment* based on elements that DON'T work for you. Remember? You've already tried all those ways that didn't work- that's why you are reading this book to begin with. If your hypothesis (based on the question above) is anything other than a big "HELL YEA!" you might want to reconfigure your plan.

* **TESTING (THE ACTUAL EXPERIMENT)**: This is where you focus on reaching something very SPECIFIC during the course of the Experiment and include elements that fit in well with YOUR current life- not elements that completely TAKE OVER your life. Those types of plans

are never sustainable and often leave you feeling miserable.
★ **ANALYSIS:** Was my hypothesis correct. AKA...Did this work for ME and MY life?
★ **CONCLUSION**: Utilize the analysis and new field research you conducted as DATA to go craft an even **better** experiment– one with even more KABAM! (scientific term of course)

In a way having an *Experiment Mentality* is like finding the ingredients to your own "magic formula" -- the one that yields you the best *results* while still enjoying the *experience* of your life. Only this time you get to fill in all the ingredients using what you know about your life-- what you like, what you don't, what works, what doesn't, etc.

You see a *real* life isn't a product of a cookie-cutter, one-size-fits-all, assembly line at a factory. That's not *real* life. A *real* life is the result of the *experiments* where you become the mad scientist set out to discover what does and doesn't work for you in your own real-world, real-life laboratory.

Bottom line: The *Factory Mentality* will almost always draw out your bitches and make it seem like your life is a comfy and cozy place for them to set down their belongings and stay a while. Become your own *Mad Scientist* and conduct your own experiments however, and those Bitches won't feel welcome for very long.

**Check out the Factory vs. Experiment Mentality Infographic in the Appendix at the back of this book.

Are You A Victim of the *Bounceback Effect*? (It's a Bitch!)

It's understandable that to some women, being promised a long-term transformation does NOT seem 'sexy' compared to things like "losing 30 pounds in 30 days".

And I can understand how pushing pause on dieting and weighing and tracking and measuring (or any form of control) to do the 'work' – – it's not sexy either. In fact it can be downright scary!

But just hear me out for a moment:

You see like clockwork I used to fill rooms with dozens of women at a time, appear on TV in front of thousands of people every single week, and teach (see also: preach) them about the importance of fitness and nutrition. I shared different ways to "drop pounds fast", "hack your motivation", or "fight your way through cravings".

The information I taught worked like gangbusters.

Pounds were dropped. Physiques were chiseled. And life-changing was happening right before my very eyes.

But here's what I was also seeing (the truth that most won't admit)

- ★ Short term 'Rah-rah'
- ★ A ton of calculating, eyeball watching, judging, and obsessing

- ★ As well as me feeling like I was 'stuck' playing the food police, their cheerleader, someone's drill sergeant, or a therapist when my clients' scale weight went up, the inches came back, or they felt exactly how they did when they met me – – sometimes even worse.

Things were great for 30 days or 6 weeks, but what happened after that?

That dreaded 'Bounceback Effect'...over and over again.

Looking back I know exactly why it happened.

We only made over PART of them. We didn't do what needed to be done on the inside. The head work, the heart work, and creating actual brain-change.

When it comes to you I want you to have BOTH parts (and if I could only choose one, I would (of course) be biased in choosing the "inner game", but I digress...)

Because here's what I know happens if you only address one side of it:

- ★ It's temporary
- ★ To be 'on', you've always got to be 'on' – – it's all or nothing
- ★ It addresses the symptoms – – everything being caused by what's going on inside

As opposed to:

- ★ Finding a permanent solution to your struggles (even if it appears to be 'slower')

★ Addressing the causes that are STRESSING you out, WEARING you out, and keeping you too BURNED out to follow through on the commitment that you made in the first place

★ Addressing the causes that are causing you to (for example) eat when you're not even hungry, eat when you're stressed, eat when you're bored, or eat when you're lonely or unhappy...

★ Addressing the causes that are causing you to stay on the couch and 'waste time' on your phone when you would rather be doing something else that would make you feel powerful, responsible, and like you're the one in 'control' of your life.

★ And finding something that actually makes you FIND happiness... now, and while you get 'there'

So to some women, a 6-month or year-long transformation seems way too long. They want results now –even if they aren't "for keeps". I can totally understand and appreciate that. But here's the thing:

If you DO want those permanent, long-term, get-them-and-KEEP-them kind of results, at some point you have to STOP doing what you know isn't working and try a different approach -- one that begins with the end in mind of what you REALLY want.

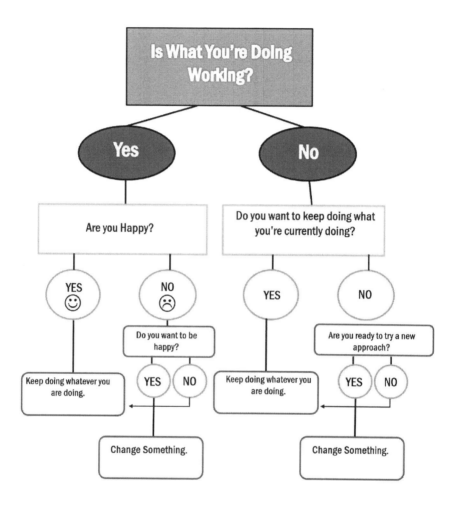

You Don't Need More Motivation

- **Motivation:** (as taken from the Distinction-ary): The driving force behind change is derived from external sources
- **Inspiration:** (as taken from the Distinction-ary): The driving force behind change is derived from within

Do you have those Bitches hanging around that convince you to quit, throw in the towel, or *"just give up now"*?

Do you get started with excitement, determination, and pep in your step only to fizzle out a few days, weeks, or willpower-tests later?

Or do you feel like your accountability, willpower, and motivation taps are always running low in fuel?

If you fall into any of the above categories, you don't need more motivation! In fact I'm going to venture to say that the amount of motivation you've been seeking and finding up until this point is the culprit in the "not finishing what I start" situations we find ourselves in (yea, I struggle with this one too.) I believe this random ramble from my Facebook page says it all perfectly.

A Ramble from the Interwebz

No, you don't need more motivation. If Facebook and Pinterest suddenly went bye-bye, then maybe I could understand the feeling of lack in the motivation department, but in actuality motivation can be found anywhere and everywhere. But that's not even the biggest problem in my opinion. I mean, how do you go find what you aren't even looking for? Just stick with me for a minute while I play "amateur psychologist".

I hear it all the time– in fact it's probably one of the statements I hear most: *"I just can't seem to stay motivated. I'll start something and do so well, but then I just lose all motivation and go back to doing X (insert past habits and patterns here)"*

Here's the thing that most people don't understand.

Motivation Gets You Going

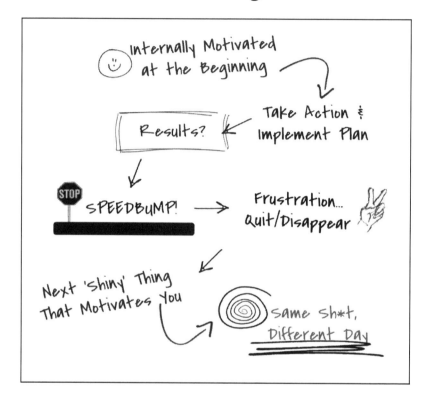

Motivation is EVERYWHERE. Motivation is easy to find. Motivation is NOT the problem.

Give me 5 minutes on Facebook and I could scroll through my newsfeed and find 10 motivational images, quotes, or articles to get my I-can-do-this juices flowing. Oh yes! And they WILL start flowing!

I might stumble upon a sexy bikini model conveniently holding a jump rope with the words; "Sweat is fat crying" or

"Abs are made in the kitchen", painted across the 3-inch square, and (for a little while) I might be motivated, go run 5 miles in the hot Florida sun or eat nothing but salad for the rest of the day.

Okay cool, I got myself a little motivation, and it KEPT me motivated...until it didn't anymore. I was good to go until I realized that I HATE running and I like to eat! Eating salads day in, day out just isn't something that I can upkeep.

Okay, so now what? I MUST be lacking motivation right? I just need to go find a little bit more! (Insert image of crack junkie with the *shake shakes* begging for just "one more fix"!)

Uber-Important distinction time! (Definitions compliments of the interwebz)

- **Motivation** – induced or incentivized human behavior
- **Inspiration** – Stimulation of the mind or emotions to a high level of feeling or activity; the act of drawing in.

My definitions/distinctions: Motivation will always be driven by an external force and will forever be fleeting and expendable. You've heard me refer to the 3rd-party Goggles, right? Those go hand-in-hand with motivation.

Inspiration Keeps You Going

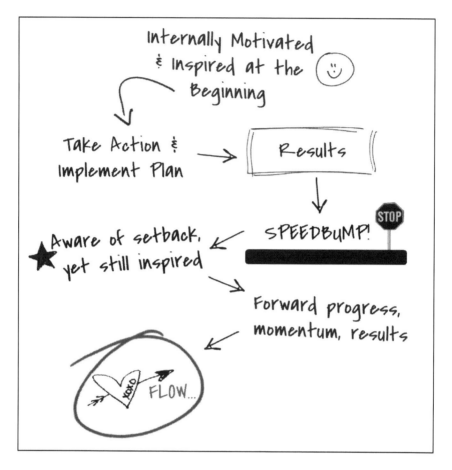

Inspiration comes from within based on the truth about what truly moves you. It has nothing to do with anything or anyone else other that what you truly want or desire. Motivation gets you going. Inspiration KEEPS you going after the motivation has faded.

★ Inspiration is what keeps you on path even when initial momentum has faded and things start to get really hard.

* Inspiration is what keeps you focused on your goal even when staying course feels uncomfortable or there's resistance.
* Inspiration is what will get you right back on track even if you stumble, encounter a speed bump, or feel like giving up.

So no, I don't believe that lack of motivation is really the problem, and I don't think you need more of it.

You don't need more mantras, options, or solutions. You don't need more pick-me-ups, motivators, or "correct" answers. I believe you simply need to start asking yourself better questions!

1. What do YOU want?
2. How do YOU want to look and feel about yourself... and your life?
3. What gets you so 'lit up' that motivation would be nice along the journey. but nothing (not a saber-tooth tiger, impending hurricane, or better option) could take your eye off that proverbial 'prize' you so desire, because you have true and utter INSPIRATION?

The Games Bitches Play

We don't typically set out to make changes to our lifestyle when we are feeling on top of the world and completely satisfied. No way!

If we want to lose weight, we might wait until we are so SICK of living a certain way-- so SICK of our clothes fitting too tightly-- so SICK of feeling like crap when we have to go shopping or slip into a bathing suit.

We wait until we are absolutely at our wits end of feeling less than we want to feel.

We wait until our plates are as full as they can be, our burdens are maxed out, and we are stressed to the gills-- until this 'problem' we are trying to solve is essentially like the "icing on the cake".

Then we might take the latest restrictive diet, insane workout routine, or some other habit-upgrading tactic we can't stand to stick to for more than a few days, and we pile it on top of our already chaotic and stressful lives.

Duh! Of course we don't have the capacity, the strength, or the willpower to possibly succeed like we really want to.

But this wasn't always so obvious to me. I continued to use plans that (when my logic brain looked at it) were setting me up to fail.

This is what I refer to as a *Losing Game*.

We know how this story goes. We know that history has a way of repeating itself. We know what happens when you try the same thing over and over again and expect different results.

Avoiding a *Losing Game*

We already talked about setting yourself up for a *Losing Game*. It's essentially setting yourself up for failure with a game plan that doesn't make sense in YOUR life. But how can you determine whether or not you are indeed playing a game designed to make you FAIL?

Here are some key points:

- ★ If you constantly feel like you are battling yourself, you're playing a *Losing Game*
- ★ If you have to overhaul your life to make it work or hate the experience as you go, you're playing a *Losing Game*
- ★ If you're constantly feeling exhausted or burnt out, you're playing a *Losing Game*
- ★ If you're still working towards achieving that SAME goal day in, day out and STILL staying STUCK, you're playing a *Losing Game*
- ★ If you're constantly looking for a 'better' plan or a new program and abandoning your current plan at the drop of a hat, you're playing a *Losing Game*
- ★ If you're still living your life going back and forth between 'on the wagon' or 'off the wagon', you're playing a *Losing Game*

If you are playing a *Losing Game*, stop what you are doing right now! Stop repeating the same mistakes and falling into the same failure-driven habits! Stop doing the same thing over and over again and expecting different results!

Not only does it not even work for you, but when you have these kinds of experiences, you get taken so far out of your flow that you reach the point where you just want to give up!

You're tired, cranky, and feel like you need a vacation from your life.

And it's usually when you are out of our flow that you are told (or volunteer yourself) to pile on extra duties, restrictions, and confinements.

Of course you fail. Of course you give up. It's a Losing Game.

But here's the other side of it: Every time you make a promise to yourself and WITNESS yourself not following through or letting yourself 'off the hook', it damages your Self-Esteem!

That 'know, like, trust' factor – you end up believing yourself less and less every single time this happens. You are actually better off NOT making the promises in the first place unless you are sure you can keep them. That's just one of the ways you can set yourself up for a 'Winning Game'.

How to Play a *Winning Game*

Imagine what your life would look like if you took the following approach instead:

Imagine if you were always playing a *Winning Game* where you always have your *flow*. *Flow* is that state of mind where you feel like your life just works. Everything feels easy and refreshing and fun. You find yourself full of energized focus and you actually enjoy the process of whatever it is you are doing. Momentum comes easily, successes come automatically, and life just seems to run smoothly — to flow.

You're not constantly hitting your head up against a wall, and you don't struggle or find internal resistance at every corner. You don't have to constantly try to talk yourself into 'it' and you're not endlessly looking for the next thing that's going to motivate you or keep you accountable.

Most ladies have never seen things through this type of lens before— that getting anything you want-- from losing weight to becoming confident and full of self-esteem isn't just a matter of willpower, desire, and hard work. In fact, I believe it's actually a matter of acquiring a basic skill set: How to run your own real-world 'Experiment' to help you get whatever you want.

And I believe that as soon as you stop approaching your goals like you were a factory-created exact replica of every other woman in the world, you're going to find that suddenly you don't feel so lost or stuck, suddenly you don't even need to rely on willpower or accountability, and suddenly you'll start actually enjoying the experience of your life while you get there.

THAT is a *Winning Game.* But you've got to set yourself up to win! How do you do that?

- ★ Only make the promises you WANT to make
- ★ Choose commitments that won't overhaul your entire life – that fit within the constraints of your life.
- ★ How you feel MATTERS! Don't commit to the things that stress you out, wear you out, bum you out, or cause you to hate your experience of life while you do it.
- ★ As yourself: Is this feasible? Will I do this? Will I enjoy this?
- ★ Bottom Line: Become a better promise-maker and a better promise-keeper.

> **RANDOM RAMBLES FROM LEANNE:** If you decided you wanted to buy a goldfish to keep as a pet, you wouldn't rearrange your entire house, change your work schedule, call your friends to tell them you won't be seeing them as much, and tell your realtor to start keeping an eye out for a bigger house? Not even close! I used to make the mistake of trying to make changes to my life that COMPLETELY uprooted my life simply because I thought that's what I "should" be doing. Those are the changes that aren't sustainable and rarely last. Make upgrades to your life that are fitting for YOUR life, what YOU want, and what feels right to YOU. You'll be amazed at how many of your "uphill battles'" start to seem like a cake walk.

A Note about Perfectionism (From A Recovering Perfectionist)

Perfectionists often wear perfectionism like a badge of honor (heck, I did for most of my life).

But I've learned that perfectionism is a weapon in disguise. Do not let it fool you.

Perfect literally means: *"to bring to full development"*.

Can we all just agree that you are never doing anything at your absolute full FULL potential?

There will always be a better, faster, easier, or more perfect way to do something -- especially if you are a growth-oriented whoa-man like you and I are.

But that's not the only thing I learned from all my years of attempting to be overly perfectionist-ic. I also learned that...

It kept me from living my life!

It kept me from getting off the sidelines, getting in the game, and trying stuff out.

In turn I created a habit of waiting, "getting ready to get ready", planning, preparing, outlining, and plotting.

A lot of saying and not as much doing.

A lot of wishing, but also a lot of waiting.

So what if we agreed on a new definition of perfect (the real definition)?

That you will never be at your 'full development' until the day you die!

That you you are evolved, evolving, and an evolution of your best self and your best life.

You are always evolving. Don't let impatience rob you of your now experiences because of your hurry to get there.

You are also more evolved than you probably give yourself credit for, so dust yourself off, get up, and just keep on practicing BEing her.

You are also a constant and never-ending evolution of your best self and your best life – – gathering stories and experiences and connections as you go. It never truly ends.

So how about in the meantime, you just go do your best, keep focusing on developing yourself into the person that would do it even more perfect-er (real word) the next time.

And because I know lifelong perfectionists don't just suddenly change overnight, let me give you some insight that might help:

Be Perfect-ish.

What I really mean is be particular about what really matters to you. Get clear on what you really want, prefer, and the things you do want to spend more focused attention on, and by all means, spend a lot of time and attention and energy on those things. Go do your best!

But get off the sidelines! Stop waiting for things to be perfect! Go get out there. Fall down. Get a bit messy. Take some wrong turns. Take the lessons and try again if it's something you really want.

But drop the "I am a perfectionist" label as a badge of honor, because it's keeping you from living your life. And it's not a label that (I believe) is serving you.

From one recovering perfectionist to another: Be okay with perfect-ish ☺

Perfectly Flawed

Here's the truth:

I'm not perfect – not by a long shot. Just like you, I am human.

- ★ Sometimes I don't follow through on the promises I make to myself.
- ★ Sometimes I start things and don't finish them.
- ★ Sometimes I fall victim to my 'bad' habits or patterns.
- ★ Sometimes I still forget that I don't really want to be perfect.
- ★ Sometimes I call myself ugly names that I know aren't really true.
- ★ Sometimes I judge myself, blame myself, feel shame of my past, fear for my future, beat myself up, treat myself harshly, or stand in my own way of getting what I want.
- ★ Every single day of my life I struggle to make the choices I need to make to keep growing and changing, and I have to **choose** to be that version of myself even when my true self wants to:

- ★ Pull the covers back over my head and shut the world out for a while
- ★ "Eat my feelings" and eat all the things that probably shouldn't be consumed in the mass quantity that I might opt for
- ★ Give up. Throw in the towel. Call it quits. (Yes! I get pushed to my edge too!)

Like I said before: Just like you, I'm human, and I became human for all the same reasons that you became human.

It's called life.

And just like you, I had to figure out how to get myself to do the things I want to do to go make myself happy– whether it was weight loss, food stuff, feeling confident and beautiful and believing in myself– whatever it was.

I couldn't just know about it. I had to KNOW about it– had to experience it as it played out in *real* life, the *real* world, and with *real* circumstances. That's what made the difference between knowing something and KNOWING something.

Bitch-Proof Habits:

Are you controlling the Bitches, or are the Bitches controlling you?

Are you being *responsible*?

Just to be clear, when I say *responsible*, I am referring to the literal definition of the word:

Literal Definition: "ability to respond, answerable, accountable for one's actions"

My Personal Interpretation: taking ownership of your life by taking your circumstances and situations and intentionally responding to them in a proactive (not reactive) way – a way that serves the life you wants to live and enables you to go take more and more control of your life.

So, do you *react* to your life? Or do you act in *response* to your life?

Often time people don't notice the difference between responding to something and reacting to something. Both require an action, and both are usually instigated by a situation or cause outside of you. But the difference between the two can actually change the circumstances quite dramatically.

And you can be sure that when you are reacting to your life and situations, the bitches are sure to be close by.

The difference between responding versus reacting can actually take a bad situation and make it worse... or it can take a bad situation and make it better....or anything in between. It's THAT game-changing.

But the key thing when it comes to both is simply realizing the distinction between the two-- and how much more in control of the *bitches* you will feel if you start *responding* more and *reacting* less.

First, let's look at the actual definitions of the two words:

Literal Definitions

- **React** -- to behave or change in a certain way when something happens
- **Respond** -- to reply or answer

My Definitions:

- **React** -- to act without thinking (unconsciously) in relation to something else.
- **Respond** -- to act with thought and intention (consciously) in relation to something else

In other words, it's a matter of being *proactive* vs. *reactive* about what you are doing, saying, being, and how you are living. One includes having control over your life and your environment, and one denotes your life and environment having control over you.

Which one do you think is a recipe for *Bitchery*? And which is a recipe for *Ditchery*?

Neither one is a "good" thing or a "bad" thing, but one way will definitely get you to your goals and the other way will send you... well... the other way.

So what do YOU do the majority of the time? How are you living YOUR life?

→   Are you intentionally and consciously living your life? Or are you just letting whatever circumstances that come your way decide? Perhaps you always go for the most accessible or convenient way?

→   Are you taking responsibility for what you happens in your day-to day life, or are you letting situations, circumstances, or other people take the blame for what you are doing?

There's inevitably going to be times in your life when you have no choice but to react (hello Saber-tooth tiger!), but if you can get better and better every single day at responding instead of reacting, it'll rock your world.

★ You'll feel more able to influence your own life.

- ★ You won't feel powerless against even the toughest obstacles.
- ★ You'll get the results you truly desire.

Here's an example of three different possible outcomes that could take place as a result of feeling "tired" in the morning, and acting accordingly:

Scenario 1: *"I was so tired this morning, so I pressed the snooze button, went back to sleep, and missed my morning workout. I felt so guilty all day"*

Scenario 2: *"I was so tired this morning, so I pressed the snooze button, went back to sleep, and missed my morning workout. I am so glad I did that. I felt amazing all day because of it. Sleep was definitely the priority this morning."*

Scenario 3: *"I was so tired this morning, but I didn't the snooze button. Instead I got out of bed, did my morning workout, and felt amazing all day!"*

None of these scenarios is "good" or "bad", "right" or "wrong". But you know how the story ends. You know how you want to FEEL in the situations that you keep re-living over and over again. You DO have the power to respond (instead of react). But you also have the power to STOP making promises to yourself that you don't REALLY want to keep. You have more power and choices than you might be recognizing.

Tightening the Leash

The act of responding requires looking at the circumstance, identifying the problem or situation, and actually trying to reconcile what is happening. That reflection can be for a moment, five seconds, one hour, two days or longer. The time frame doesn't matter. What matters is that you stopped and put an effort to think and suspend judgment. Yes, it takes conscious effort in the beginning, but it shows that you are willing to listen and observe and figure out what the heck is going on.

Reacting on other hand is the absence of this time gap. It is an immediate behavioral response and it is usually based upon emotions and not intellect.

This 'gap' between the circumstance and your behavior is the key to your success and what ultimately leads you to gaining a sense of 'control'. Once you can identify what's actually going on, then you can make choices in *response* to the situation-- not in *reaction*. The key is that pause.

If the situation does in fact require immediate action (like maybe you forgot your lunch, or you are put on the spot at work to give a presentation), then just take a deep breath first. This alone can help you gain a feeling of control and calmness so you can make the choice that serves you best.

Great question to ask yourself during that pause:

> *"How will this make me FEEL? Will this make me a better version of myself?"*

Or (depending on the situation), I might ask myself:

> *"Will I [feel like crap/beat myself up/have a lot of guilt] after this?"*

Just doing this alone, you'll start easily making the "right" choices.

Upgrading Your Habits

When was the last time you set out to do something, and it went exactly as you planned? Almost never.

Most things never go down exactly as we plan it, because we aren't psychic-- we have no idea what's going to go on in the future-- especially when a lot of the variables are out of our control.

And it's usually those unforeseen curveballs that enter our life that get us off track, or throw us for a loop, or create a setback.

It's important to understand distinction between setback and failure.

"Successful people are a result of not just the awesome habits they create and their relentless drive and determination to see things through to the end-- it's more a matter of how well they handle setbacks." – Unknown

And setbacks are inevitable.

Think of all the times in your life that one or all of the following happened:

You were in the zone in all elements of your life, and BAM! Something unexpected came up in your life and all your previous 'flow' went out the window.

Or even things like paying off an old debt and then all of a sudden you need a cavity filled and it's $1000 or you get in a car accident and it's a $500 deductible.

Or maybe you're on a 'clean eating' plan, but you get the flu! Sure, you feel lean and skinny after you've been throwing up for 2 days, but now all you can stomach to eat is crackers and egg McMuffins and Gatorade, and you all of a sudden feel squishy and have crazy cravings for crap -- let alone now having no energy to work out. All of a sudden you're now "off the wagon".

Or maybe you're doing great on a project and BAM the variables change, or you lose a team member, or the client changes what they want.

These are all setbacks!

"But that wasn't part of the plan!"

Yes, I know it wasn't. But the one thing I can guarantee that IS part of the plan is that there are NO guarantees about how the course of events in your life will pan out. The only thing you can count on is THAT: Curveballs, unexpected circumstances, and setbacks WILL keep happening! You will be continually thrown off course.

But how you choose to deal with them is the deciding factor in whether or not you can stick to what you committed to in the first place.

"Opposition is a natural part of life. Just as we develop our physical muscles through overcoming opposition - such as lifting weights - we develop our character muscles by overcoming challenges and adversity."

- Stephen Covey

Are you flexing your 'overcoming setback' *muscles*?

It's time to take your REAL life into account so you can set yourself up with REAL expectations, and set realistic goals that will carry you through to your mission. Only then can you go create realistic parameters, guidelines, and deadlines to get you there.

If we shy away from the 'hope everything goes perfectly' mindset and simply replace with the assumption that our plan might not go perfectly according to plan (and probably won't in fact), not only can we improve the way we handle setbacks, but in addition to that we can create a plan that actually **makes allowances** for setbacks. How's that for being prepared for curveballs?

To me, the ONLY way to set yourself up for a winning game when it comes to instilling new behaviors and habits in your life is this one.

Only then do you have the mindset you will need to commit to doing everything that you can (and are willing to do) right now.

Always Do Your Best. Your best is going to change from moment to moment; it will be different when you are healthy as opposed to sick. Under any circumstance, simply do your best, and you will avoid self-judgment, self-abuse, and regret.

– Don Miguel Ruiz

Getting A.I.R.

Okay, no doubt you've heard it takes approximately 30 days to get acclimated to a new habit in your life or to create it.

Now depending who you ask, you might hear 21 days. You might hear 30 days. Either way, it's VERY possible to neurologically fire and wire new patterns into your life VERY quickly.

The part of the 'math' that no one has the answer to though: how long it takes to condition your brain to STOP doing the old habit or pattern.

For example, a while back I realized that based on some old injuries and due to the effects of spine surgery, the entire right side of my body wasn't functioning properly, and I was using my left side WAY more.

Walking. Lunging. Carrying groceries. Balancing. Pushing a door open.
Right side was not pulling its weight.

Well you know what else I discovered after that? I wasn't BREATHING properly. My left side was doing most of the work for every breath I took as well.

When I set out to retrain my body and brain to breathe differently, it took way more repetitions than it did when I did *"The Great train-myself-to-carry-my-purse-on-the-opposite-shoulder experiment of 2011"*.

I set out to go from carrying it on my right side to my left side on a Sunday, and by Thursday I was already automatically putting it on my left shoulder. Sunday-Wednesday I would catch myself with my purse on my right shoulder and actively remove it and switch sides. By Thursday, it was an automatic reflex to wear it on my left.

Breathing however took me **months** to retrain it, and it was HARD!

Why?

How many repetitions of breathing do you complete every single minute, hour, or year? That's a lot of repetitions to UN-teach your brain!

So training a new habit is one thing, but getting yourself to stop doing the old habit is not so black and white. There's no blanket answer for how long that will take.

But I do know that the only way to do either (create a new or replace an old) is with a little bit of A.I.R.:

Attention. Intention. Repetition.

Attention- What awareness do you need to carry around with you every single day so that you become hyper-aware of what you are doing or not doing that isn't serving you? What is it *specifically* that you looking to upgrade or looking to replace and where do you see or experience it showing up in your life? What specifically do you need to be focusing on (or be aware of) in order to create the changes you need to upgrade this specific habit? Awareness is a key factor in attention.

Intention- Where (and in which direction) do you want to head, and where are you looking? What do you *want* to do? And what are you actually *committing* to? Or where do you want to head in addition to the destination you are already heading. Remember, there's a MASSIVE difference in the outcome of where your airplane ends up if you buy a ticket to Kansas vs. buying a ticket to Dublin. Intention allows you to design the specific *direction* of the outcome that you want these changes to lead you to.

Repetition- We are all creatures of habit. For reasons and scientific "Geekery" beyond the scope of this section, let's just say that our brains are physiologically and emotionally wired to repeat patterns of behaviors. In order to establish new patterns, the new behaviors (aka the changes you want to make) need to be established and engrained through repetition.

Before You Upgrade

Where are you right now?

If you went online to buy an airplane ticket, and only typed in the destination only, the website wouldn't let you advance to the next page. As long as you kept the origin location left blank, the website wouldn't be able to do its job.

Flying to Denver from L.A. is completely different than flying to Denver from Tokyo. Different routes, different coordinates. Different destinations. In fact it would change the experience of your trip completely. They are two different places.

In order to figure out what route you need to take to get where you want to go, you must first figure out where you are starting from.

Where Do You Want To Be?

This is the part that most people often skip over. Often times we want to feel productive and accomplished, so we just fill out time with 'work'. The problem is though that this can leave us to actually flounder and get nowhere fast (or worse), somewhere we don't want to be. Before you hit the gas, decide which direction you want the vehicle to head and where you want to end up.

How Will You Get There?

I learned from my days in the fitness industry after prescribing the "right" way and the "wrong" way for years on end that there is no "right" way—there's only the right way for YOU. Hence my take on *experiments*.

What do you think happened when I prescribed meal plans that contained broccoli and salmon to someone that HATED broccoli and salmon? You think they stuck it out very long? Unbeknownst to me I was actually setting up my clients for a *Losing Game.*

To me, a *Winning Game* is one that you can play that actually allows you to enjoy your experience of life while still getting results. It also incorporates your REAL life. We talked about curveballs and setbacks earlier. You'll dramatically decrease your risk of those if you keep your preferences and your lifestyle in mind which creating your plan.

Are You Bitching Or Ditching?

Sometimes there's things in our lives we don't love.

They can frustrate us, annoy us, or downright piss us off.

And sometimes those 'things' are outside of our control. As in there's nothing we can do about it.

At that point though, we still have a choice:

★ We can choose to focus on what we DON'T like, what we DON'T want more of, or what we DON'T have....

-OR-

★ We can focus on what we DO want, what we DO like, what we DO have, and what we DO have influence over.

I find myself caught up in my own cycles of 'stuckness' all the time. And I can guarantee you that when I get REALLY stuck inside of it, it's because I'm BITCHING, complaining, or focusing on everything that's outside of my control and influence.

★ I go into problem-seeking mode instead of solution-seeking mode.
★ I focus on what I don't have vs what I could (and arguably 'should') feel grateful for in my life.
★ I feel things like self-pity, self-loathing, or self-blame...instead of doing whatever it takes to FIND my power, FIND my focus, and FIND the love that I know is in my heart.

And I continue to do this until I have that moment where I say:

"Okay Leanne, so what's next? You can sit here complaining, bitching, and feeling like crap....OR you can go focus on what you can do RIGHT now to get yourself out of 'the shit'."

And that's when I realize (see also: remember) that I DO have a choice. We always have a choice.

So here's what I say about it now:

FEEL that frustration. Don't ignore that the 'thing' downright SUCKS or upsets you.

Feel all 'the feels'. Then ask yourself:

"Is this something I can actually go do something about? Or is this out of my 'control'?"

Or...another question might be:

"What CAN I do to influence myself, my circumstances, and how I feel RIGHT NOW?"

Either way, I guarantee that you DO have a choice as to what you do or don't do in any given moment, in any given situation.

So what will you choose? (And choosing to do NOTHING and repeat the cycle of stuckness is still a choice).

When 'shit hits the fan', what are you going do? Bitch about it? Or ditch the cycle of stuckness that's keeping you 'in' it?

It's your choice, whether you own it or not.

But as soon as you do start to own that you are the one (and only one) with the most powerful influence over your life, EVERYTHING will change for you. EVERYTHING.

A Recap (And Where to Go From Here)

Once you start looking for them, it's easy to see where Bitches are showing up in your life, stealing your confidence and your smiles, and making all the decisions for you without your conscious permission.

As you read *How to Ditch the Bitch*, you may have even been able to detect which types of Bitches are showing up the most in your own life.

And we ALL have bitches (or so I believe).

They may have different names, different faces, and come out in different circumstances, but here's what's always true:

We all have our own special blend and own special 'recipe'.

We can either fight them, believe them, resist them, or ignore them. Or we can accept that they are indeed there and that:

★ They bring a story with them (THEY bring the drama)
★ They are your unfair and unkind judgements about yourself (and the judgements will never go away, but being mindful of the kind of judgements you're making (kind vs. fair)
★ They are *Ditch*-able! As in, you can become the version of yourself that isn't so impacted by them, and YOU can become the version of yourself that has **the most** influence over your life and how you feel.

Here's what you can do NOW and moving forward:

1. Accept that YOU have Bitches and get to know them. (This book is the first step in doing just that.) Create new *Awareness Awarenesses* -- and really start getting to understand them and (in turn) understand YOU! Don't fight them. Don't resist them. And don't try to mentally 'kill' them. Start being of where of them and what they are saying. Then start to decipher what they are ACTUALLY saying.
2. Know them and seek to understand them.
3. Take these new *Awareness Awarenesses* and let them permeate into the inner-workings of your brain. And then go and influence YOU. Influence who you're being, what you're doing, and how you're feeling by getting yourself involved in a *Winning Game* Plan with *Winning* Experiments -- one that's designed for the individual that you are, not for the 'widget' that you're not.
4. Go about the 'business' of your life with all of your new *Awareness Awarenesses* -- especially how you're talking **to** yourself, **about** yourself.

That's it! (Simple, but not always easy!)

Don't worry though. I've got you covered. In addition to all of the clarity-seeking questions I have provided throughout this book, I've made it really easy for you to start Ditching YOUR Bitches and continue on your journey.

The place to start is with my 'Reality Check'.

I've created a series of questions (and more specific Awarenesses) to help you start UNDERSTANDING your Bitches. If you simply answer the questions I've provided as thoughtfully and honestly as possibly, it would be impossible to NOT create the new *Awareness Awarenesses* that you need in your mind and in your brain to move forward and start Ditching YOUR Bitches.

You'll also get access to my *Distinction-ary* so you can gain even MORE insight into the Ditch the Bitch perspective on making over your Self-Talk and BodyTalk moving forward.

These 10+ distinctions that are in the Distinction-ary will give you a new pair of 'goggles' with which to see yourself, your struggles, and your ever-evolving always-growing life experience. You can gain access to all of this and more over on this special page on my website:

www.LeanneEllington.com/HTDTB

In addition I've included an Appendix on the following pages with resources that will continue to help you Ditch Your Bitches.

I recommend that you go through these to immediately gain new clarity on the *Bitchery* showing up in your life, and how you can start on the road to *Ditchery* right away.

Good luck, and happy Bitch-Ditching!

www.LeanneEllington.com/HTDTB

DITCHifesto

DEFINITIONS & DISTINCTIONS

Perfectionism: The perception of what you do as being right or wrong, good or bad. You can't be real as long as you're worried about being perfect. Taking risks is impossible if you're paralyzed by fear of failure.

Language: You do not need to live your live your life by other people's definitions of words. You can create your own language based on your own knowledge, feelings, and beliefs at any time you wish.

Belief: What you know to be true (about yourself or anything else) can be completely different tomorrow. Confidence & self-image are a product of how you feel about yourself.

Inspiration: The driving force behind change is derived from within

Motivation: The driving force behind change is derived from external sources

The Life I Love: A result of falling in love with the person you *are*, accepting and believing in who you are, and trusting who you show up as every single day. Being happy, excited, and content, so you can live with passion and purpose—not excuses. Having the courage, the confidence, and the power to decide who you want to be RIGHT NOW.

Awesome: Exceptional, amazing, and supportive of your

goals.

Respond: My life is dictated by the momentum of my actions.

React: Actions dictated by the momentum of my life.

Speed Bumps: Unforeseen setbacks that are completely out of your control. Illness, opposition, challenges, or adversity.

Change: Alter what you are *doing*

Transform: Alter who you are *being*

Experiments: You can't learn what provides the best balance of results and quality of life by learning it from someone else, you have to *experience* it for yourself. What do you need? What do you like? What don't you like? What is helpful? Be your own mad scientist. Use your past experiences as data (not failures) to help you create your own winning combination.

Habits:

Automatic, unconscious behaviors ingrained through repetition. They're going to happen with or without your intention.

Being Real: Showing up as your true, authentic self.

APPENDIX

Are You *Ditching* or *Bitching*?

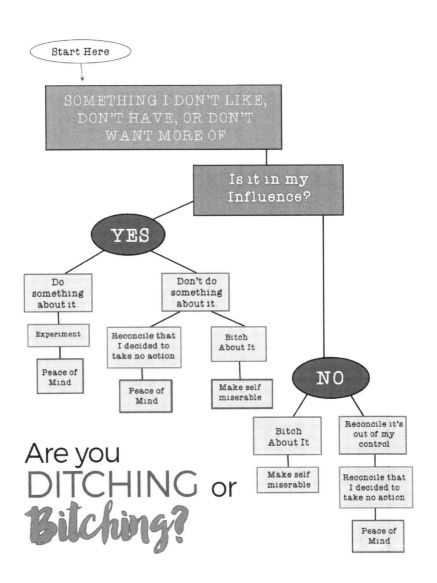

Are You Making Noise or Music?

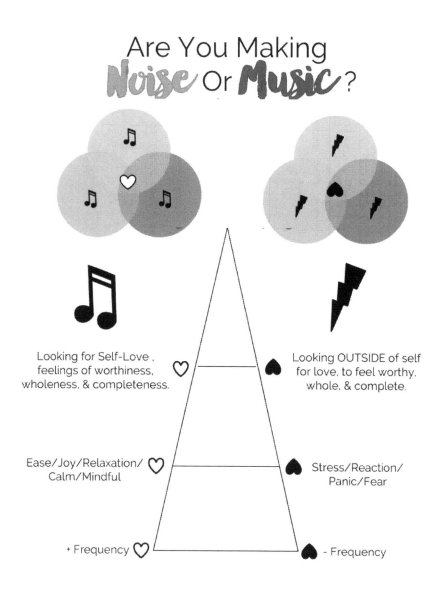

Ditchery-Do's

Ditchery-Do's

1. Show up, be seen, and don't apologize for who you are.
2. Change your beliefs by changing the words you use <u>to</u> yourself <u>about</u> yourself.
3. Become the most confident woman you know by becoming your biggest cheerleader.
4. Change your habits quickly by first focusing on what you need to STOP doing.
5. Create whatever body would enhance your ability to live a life you love and never diminish it.
6. Know the difference between what happened and what you say about what happened.
7. Upgrade your self-esteem by keeping more promises to yourself. Keep more promises to yourself by only making promises you want to keep.
8. Focus on what you DO have, DO like, and DO want more of. Figure out what lights you up and use THAT as motivation and inspiration.
9. When you don't fully feel in control, see where you can react less and respond more.
10. Start regarding failures and setbacks as valuable currency and data.

Bitchery Clues

Bitchery Clues

1. Life is being seen through 3rd-party judgment goggles.
2. You are shrinking yourself or not showing up as the best version of yourself --the REAL you.
3. You are unfairly criticizing or judging your actions or words.
4. You are focusing more on WHAT to do rather than HOW you do what you do.
5. You aren't enjoying the EXPERIENCE of how your body looks, moves, or feels.
6. You are reacting instead of responding, and life seems to be running YOU.
7. You're doing whatever you think you are "supposed to" or whatever is "right" or "good".
8. You are constantly looking for a drip-feed of motivation to get you going or keep you going.
9. You're STUCK and afraid to move in one direction or the other or worried how you think it might be received.
10. You're focusing on what you DON'T want, DON'T have, or DON'T want more of. You are focusing on the PROBLEM instead of the SOLUTION.

Factory vs. *Experiment* Mentality

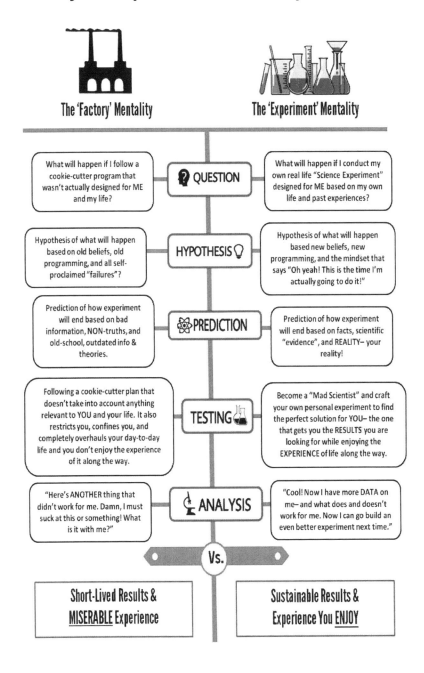

The 'Factory' Mentality · The 'Experiment' Mentality

QUESTION

What will happen if I follow a cookie-cutter program that wasn't actually designed for ME and my life?

What will happen if I conduct my own real life "Science Experiment" designed for ME based on my own life and past experiences?

HYPOTHESIS

Hypothesis of what will happen based on old beliefs, old programming, and all self-proclaimed "failures"?

Hypothesis of what will happen based new beliefs, new programming, and the mindset that says "Oh yeah! This is the time I'm actually going to do it!"

PREDICTION

Prediction of how experiment will end based on bad information, NON-truths, and old-school, outdated info & theories.

Prediction of how experiment will end based on facts, scientific "evidence", and REALITY– your reality!

TESTING

Following a cookie-cutter plan that doesn't take into account anything relevant to YOU and your life. It also restricts you, confines you, and completely overhauls your day-to-day life and you don't enjoy the experience of it along the way.

Become a "Mad Scientist" and craft your own personal experiment to find the perfect solution for YOU– the one that gets you the RESULTS you are looking for while enjoying the EXPERIENCE of life along the way.

ANALYSIS

"Here's ANOTHER thing that didn't work for me. Damn, I must suck at this or something! What is it with me?"

"Cool! Now I have more DATA on me– and what does and doesn't work for me. Now I can go build an even better experiment next time."

Vs.

Short-Lived Results & MISERABLE Experience

Sustainable Results & Experience You ENJOY

Bitch-Ditchery Map

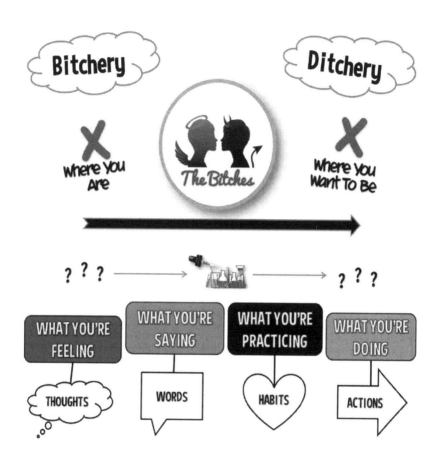

How To *Change* Your *Story*

✓ **THE STORY:**

What are your Bitches saying to you?

✓ **THE HOLES:**

Where are the lies? What's NOT true?

✓ **THE REALITY:**

Which parts are true?

✓ **A BETTER STORY:**

What do I now CHOOSE to say about it?

About The Author:

What started out as a nickname given to negative self-talking voices from the mind of researcher, writer, TV personality, entrepreneur, and creator of Ditch the Bitch Leanne Ellington, has turned into quite a revolution to help women all over the world feel more empowered, confident, and happy by taking back control of the driver's seat of their own lives. Leanne's first career endeavor was focused on the *Outer Game* of fitness and weight loss and helping women makeover their bodies and their lifestyle. It was completely fueled by her own personal desire to overcome the overweight and out of shape body that she had been carrying with her ever since childhood.

But it quickly became very apparent to Leanne that the distinction between 'losing weight" and "loving your body and your life" were two very different things. After her deep exploration of mindset, the brain, pain, and inner self-talk and how it controls perception and experiences, she fell in love with helping women work on the *Inner Game* of their transformations. *How to Ditch the Bitch* is the first of Leanne's programs that dive into the personal development, performance, and self-improvement side of things to replace all the things in women's lives that they don't love with something extraordinary.

How to Contact Leanne Ellington:

→ FOR SPEAKING ENGAGEMENTS:

Email: Support@LeanneEllington.com

→ TO CONNECT:

Website: http://www.LeanneEllington.com

Facebook: www.facebook.com/AuthorLeanneEllington

Community: If you want to join in the conversation and connect with other fellow Bitch-Ditchers to help you along your journey, come join us over here:

https://www.facebook.com/groups/EatPlayLoveLive/

1-on-1 Help: If you know you are serious about ending your struggles, and would like help to gain the clarity, focus, and direction you need to Break OUT of the disempowering relationship you feel stuck in (but don't know what that looks like), apply for a Breakout Session with Leanne (It's free!).

http://LeanneEllington.com/apply/

Made in the USA
Columbia, SC
09 March 2021

34098384R00111